MEMOIRS
of a
TIGER

CHARLES L. BYRUM

AuthorHouse™
1663 Liberty Drive
Bloomington, IN 47403
www.authorhouse.com
Phone: 833-262-8899

Published by AuthorHouse 07/27/2023

ISBN: 979-8-8230-0995-9 (sc)
ISBN: 979-8-8230-0994-2 (e)

Print information available on the last page.

This book is printed on acid-free paper.

Cover Photo by Julie Leahy

This book is dedicated to the late Bill Fox,
a teammate in high school and in college,
and an excellent player and blocker.

CHAPTER 1

STARTERS

I SHOWED UP IN THIS WORLD in September of 1944 in San Antonio, Texas, where my father was stationed as a pilot in the US Air Force at Fort Sam Houston. He, just twenty-four, and my mother, twenty-two and pregnant, greeted me while my father recovered from a midair collision he'd experienced in training that had caused him to be released from active duty.

My folks proceeded to make the long drive home from Texas to Evanston, Illinois, where both of them had grown up. My father had no particular skills that had prepared him for employment, but he was a confident young man and was very persuasive. He soon decided to interview for a sales position with Conover-Mast Publications, publisher of a trade magazine that advertised construction equipment. It didn't hurt that the owner of Conover-Mast was the father of his good friend from high school, Bud Mast. Dad got the sales job, and it was a perfect fit for him.

Upon their arrival in Evanston, my folks soon proceeded to increase the family to five kids and moved to the neighboring town of Wilmette, located on the shores of beautiful Lake Michigan. As a result of the move, their two boys and three girls were enrolled at Avoca School in Wilmette, where they began thriving.

I soon developed a fondness for sports—especially football, which I played pretty well. It was a very positive experience for me because of the social advantages and confidence it gave me. You could say that I blossomed at Avoca while playing football against teams from other schools.

My progress in football was not helped as much as it could have been by Avoca's football coach, Irving Kuklin, who ran not only the football program but also the woodshop at Avoca for the period I was there. While surrounding schools regularly played each other, Kuklin's program was limited to intramural games between teams from the seventh and eighth grades where there was no instruction in blocking, tackling, or running plays. Pads, helmets, and shoes were purchased by the players' families at Sears, Roebuck, and Company, not at the higher-end local sporting goods stores servicing the other teams when they suited up for games.

As a result, a large percentage of the football players on the Avoca teams soon quit the sport, leaving only a handful to go out for the football team as freshmen at New Trier, the local high school. It included few players who had been trained in Kuklin's grab-ass system, which had no skills, no playbook, and no coaching. I'd still enjoyed it and wanted more, so I looked forward to New Trier.

On one midsummer Sunday as my father grilled charburgers, a family favorite, he dropped a bombshell: his company had hired him to run its sales program from its New York City office. We would be moving to Larchmont, a town in New York, and I would be attending Mamaroneck High School (MHS), not New Trier, as I had looked forward to. The move had no effect on my sisters and was OK with my brother, but I was devastated. At this point in my life, it was the worst thing that could happen to me. I was leaving the kids I had gone to school with up to that point. *No more neighborhood friends, and maybe*, I thought, *no more football*. I didn't know if they even played it there.

The remainder of the summer was tough for me to handle. Soon, our house was sold, the whole family jumped into our station wagon, and everyone waved their goodbyes to Wilmette with tears in their eyes. Looking back at the Chicago Skyway as we left town made me realize this was really happening.

At my first day of school in Mamaroneck as a new kid, I was the major point of interest for the members of my class. I could tell right away I wasn't in Wilmette anymore. The kids in my new school did not understand my manner of speech, and I, in return, did not understand theirs. I was placed in a seat between two girls who spoke English well enough, but their thick New York accents completely threw me out of sync when we started to converse. I thought I was in another world when I first started talking to them, and at the same time, they laughed at everything I said.

It was all good-natured exchanges, but it was confusing for both sides. While they said they "sore" my history book and could "heah" what I had to say, they laughed at everything I said, which I thought was perfectly normal. I was glad that I continued to sit with them because I began to understand them, and they started to understand me. Eventually, we all thought the conversations between us were cordial and understandable.

A large number of my new classmates in Mamaroneck were immigrants and had trouble speaking English. This was easier for them than for me because no one was expected to understand one another, and everyone was spared embarrassment. After a while, the ability to communicate improved both ways. I was comfortable that I would fit in, and as it turned out, I did.

One of the things I enjoyed when I went to a bilingual classmate's home was learning how to pronounce cuss words in English to the family's native language. It wasn't very cool, but it was fun to do. These weren't common events in Chicago.

It was easier for me to succeed in football at Mamaroneck than I expected, since a large number of MHS students—and students in the schools we played—were more proficient in soccer than I was but were not so good at American football. The football advantage went to American-born players like me.

In football, Mamaroneck started out its freshman teams running the T formation since it was the easiest to learn and execute. The freshmen who were serious about learning it had practiced in advance.

CHAPTER 2

FRESHMAN FOOTBALL AT MAMARONECK

I COULDN'T HAVE BEEN MORE THRILLED when I registered as a freshman at Mamaroneck and was told that tryouts for football would take place during the first week of school. I had no idea what to expect since I didn't know the players or how good they would be.

I soon received a flyer from the freshman football coach, Chick Talgo, stating that the team would practice every day after school from three to five o'clock until October 31. We'd play other freshmen teams in our league from Ossining, New Rochelle, Scarsdale, Rye, Portchester, Edison Tech, and Pelham during the months of September and October.

The flyer said that game uniforms and practice uniforms could be picked up on Mondays and returned to the locker room attendants on Thursdays for cleaning. The attendants would also fit the players at the first practice with jockstraps and mouthpieces. All in all, a total group of sixty anxious freshmen showed up on the first day. Ten players were trying out for quarterback, thirty for halfback or offensive end, and the rest for defense. No one tried out for the offensive line—not even the slow, overweight players. This was normal in freshman football at most schools.

Coach Talgo had been the varsity quarterback for the Tigers in his junior and senior years of high school and had gone on to be a fast-pitch wizard in the Mamaroneck softball leagues. After one day of practice, he'd assigned thirty-five of the players to first- or second-string positions, and the remaining players were designated as third-string, or worse—in the line. By the end of the first week, a total of twenty freshmen had quit and turned in the helmets, pads, shoes, and uniforms the school had given them to practice in.

The week following the mass return of uniforms by dropouts, Coach Talgo and his assistants posted the lineups of the offense and defense for the Tigers.

I was counting on my speed to help me earn a first- or second-team spot and was issued a helmet, shoulder pads, hip pads, football shoes, game and practice jerseys, and pants. All equipment had been used in prior years by earlier teams. There were fifty players who showed up on the first day for their equipment and uniforms. Half of them had played in park-district or grade-school flag football teams. The rest had not. None had played tackle football before at any level.

Coach Talgo had four assistant coaches, all with whistles to use in games and all who had some experience in coaching freshman footballers at Mamaroneck. With that, the formal opening of freshman football started, and the MHS freshman coaches busily spent their time in special sessions to teach the MHS format to incoming participants. Notices of these sessions were posted on the school bulletin boards a week in advance of the first session.

Tryouts for player positions at Mamaroneck were conducted the same way as in most high schools. Every player trying out for the team had predetermined not only the position he should play but also what the starting lineup of the freshman team should be. Some even had their pictures taken in their uniforms.

The coaches didn't announce the favorites for the positions on the team, even though they probably had their own ideas of who they were. They didn't disclose them because they wanted every player to believe he had a chance to play, in order to encourage as many as possible to try out and be discovered as a diamond in the rough. I was a new guy, and no one knew about me or my chances to make it. From observing, I guessed the chances of other players. In the process, I befriended Noel Murano, who was trying out for end, and he eagerly gave me his own assessment of candidates, which turned out to be pretty accurate because he was familiar with how Coach Talgo went about teaching the fundamentals of running, tackling, and passing. So, after a while, we got the message and did what the coach told us to do after positions were assigned and plays were taught and repeated. Best of all, I was designated to be the left halfback. After two weeks of practice, the Tigers appeared to be as ready as we could be for the opening game against our traditional rival, Scarsdale, but we still managed to have a ragtag look to us. This could be evidenced by the application of eye black under everyone's eyes prior to the game. Stickum from spray cans was also applied to the hands of players who wanted it (which turned out to be everyone, not just backs and ends). This made things a sticky mess for most players for the rest of the game. Before the game, the team elected Ronnie Hopkins (our quarterback) and Skip Murdoch (our tight end) as cocaptains for the team. Both players were good athletes and were well respected by the players.

CHAPTER 3

FOOTBALL OPENER AT MAMARONECK VERSUS SCARSDALE

Our first game was against Scarsdale, a traditional rival of Mamaroneck. We won the toss and elected to receive the opening kickoff. It was clear that we all had the jitters when the kickoff was made by Scarsdale. The two starting halfbacks for the Tigers were me and Alvin Plummer, who was also going to try out as a sprinter on the track team. Alvin had strong thighs and powerful-looking legs and looked ready to go when the whistle was blown for the kickoff.

The kickoff by the Scarsdale kicker was a strong one and was cradled in the arms of Alvin, who was standing on the Tiger fifteen-yard line, a pretty good kick.

Alvin's job, once he fielded the ball, was to catch the kick and break it in the middle of the field, then look for me, as the other designated returner, to also block for the middle and throw a block on any defender trying to get to him, so that he was in the clear. Both of us did our jobs, and it worked. I raced down toward the player who was coming across the field to get to me and enabled Alvin to get out to the fifty-yard line before he was tackled so we could start on offense, which was a great start to the game.

After two running plays by me, Hopkins threw a flat pass to Murdoch, who turned the corner and picked up a thirty-yard gain to Scarsdale's twenty. Our fullback, Benny Orsino, ran two plays up the middle and scored a touchdown. We tried to kick for the extra point, but it was blocked, so the score was six-zero Tigers, a great start. Scarsdale later scored on a running play, capping a sixty-yard drive, and Mamaroneck scored on a thirty-yard pass from Hopkins to Murano. Both teams successfully kicked their extra points.

In the final score, Mamaroneck won thirteen-seven. The Tigers whooped and jumped like we had just won a championship game; we were elated. We had won the first football game on both the offense and defense plays, and I breathed a big sigh of relief upon hearing the news that I was going to play first team offense and second team defense.

Since many players on the freshmen team were totally new to the sport of football and the requirements of the sport, we needed to grasp three things before we played in our initial game: first, the position each would play on offense or defense; second, our responsibilities on each play; and third, the physical task to be performed by each of us performing our responsibilities.

A football play starts with the snap count from the quarterback when the offensive team huddles up before a play; the quarterback tells the offensive players what number he will call when the ball is to be snapped to him. The snap starts the play, and everyone proceeds with their assignments. It takes a while for learning the process to sink in, but when it does, the play starts and the defensive team reacts to stop the play from working.

It didn't take long for Coach Talgo to make the team understand what they were supposed to do with each play and to carry out their roles during the next couple of weeks.

CHAPTER 4

PELHAM

THE MAMARONECK TIGERS FRESHMAN TEAM had a very good season following the win at Scarsdale, and this was evidenced by our game with Pelham. We had reached four wins and two losses, and the game at Pelham would be a good test. Pelham was located in Westchester County, same as Mamaroneck, and its high school team, the Pelicans, was always good. The game was to be played at Pelican Field at 4:00 p.m. on October 15, so conditions were ideal.

The Pelham freshmen had one big offensive line and four running backs who were fast and strong. Their quarterback was very ordinary, but with the size of their line and the speed of their running backs, they didn't need much of a quarterback to be effective.

As the team took the field, and I saw the size of Pelham's line, I quickly sized up our chances. The Pelham team was big and mature. A good portion of them had stubble on their faces, and a smaller percentage had actual facial hair that had already turned into mustaches and the beginnings of beards. *Damn. Those guys are beasts*, I thought as I observed the Pelicans run through the pregame warm-ups. Once we heard the referee's whistle when the play was completed, I was shocked by a forceful hit to the back of my helmet by a Pelican player. This was followed by a blast from the referee's whistle, ending the play. However, rather than throwing the penalty flag, as I had expected, the referee ran up to the pile of players and unexpectedly shouted at the tackler. "Damn it, Lennie, if you do that again, I will call a penalty and throw you out of the game." He had the same jutting jaw and hooked nose of the player I had seen warming up for Pelham. The resemblance of the referee and the Pelham player was unmistakable. The two were spitting images of one another.

The chastened look in Lennie's eyes confirmed what I had concluded from the incident, and I was sure that somewhere in Pelham that night, a player known as Lennie was atoning to an uncle, some hot-tempered relative, for his actions on the football field that day, and that his deportment would have to improve considerably for him to be of any value to the team.

We received the opening kickoff, and Plummer returned it to the Tigers' forty-yard line, a pretty good return. Coach Talgo had taught us to run a reverse the week before the game, a play where the right halfback takes a handoff from the quarterback and runs to the left side of the field and hands off to the left side, handing off to the left halfback, who runs it back to the right side. There is a lot of running with the play, so when it worked, it was for big yardage. Coach thought it was worth the try, so he sent in the signal to run it. As left halfback, it was my assignment to take the ball from the right halfback coming across, and try to run it around the right. I took the ball from Murano, who was running my way, and then I looked for Plummer coming across. He made a good handoff, and Alvin immediately looked for me to come around and grab the ball, which I did, and took it to the right side. I fought through a couple of Pelicans and picked up about fifteen yards before one of them tackled me. I was in the process of falling down and hearing that most of us never played and were hungry for more. We scored and we won.

After the two teams followed the customary ritual of shaking hands with each other at the end of the game, we piled into the bus that would take us back to our high school so we could shower and go home, and Butch Mayo, our starting tackle, started the chant: "We did it again, we did it again, we won! We won!" Soon, we all picked it up and loudly chanted all the way back until we got off the bus. It may have sounded obnoxious, but not to us.

Winning from the get-go is a real boost in a young team, and it gives them confidence they can build on. The Tigers were no exception.

The Tigers were freshmen and needed to feel that we were good, and so we continued for the better, receiving accolades from the school and the student body, like we had from beating Scarsdale. And when the team's bus rolled in, there were a dozen or so freshman girls cheering and clapping. "Criminy," exclaimed Ronnie Hopkins. "This is crazy. No one has ever done this for me or these guys before, I can tell you that." He knew this to be true, as he had grown up with most of the team.

Ronnie was a good teammate and a really good guy. He was a leader but not a shouter. I started with him in our games during freshman year, and in our sophomore year as junior varsity (JV) players when we not only were on the junior varsity roster, but we got to dress with the varsity players and sit on the bench with them in the varsity games, and we occasionally got into some of those games.

I was not only starting and playing in all of the JV games and many varsity games, but I was also thriving as a player and was a lock to complete my high school football career as a Mamaroneck Tiger, when my father took the train home from the city one night and made a startling announcement. We were "moving back to Chicago."

The family was stunned by the announcement. It was no surprise that my mother was elated by it. She had hated to leave Chicago and her friends and was distressed about how that move to New York had affected my sisters. I was perfectly happy with Mamaroneck because of the opportunities it gave me to excel in sports and to make a lot of friends at school because of sports, not to mention the fact that I had been dating a cute girl at Mamaroneck High School. That would all change with our move back to Chicago.

CHAPTER 5

CROSSING THE SOUND

ONE SATURDAY AFTERNOON, TIM ALEX (who was moored on a tackle in the team) and I were invited to take a ride with our classmate, Frank Herz, in his boat along the shore at Mamaroneck, and between the three of us, we did not figure out where to go. It was just fun riding on the Sound, on our way to Long Island. Late in the day, near dusk, the waves kicked up and the winds drove us across the Sound toward Long Island. Eventually, they swamped the boat and drove us to a point about 100 yards from the shore, where we started to sink. We had to get out of the boat and walk in the water to a point on the beach where we could ground the boat after making our way through the waves. By divine intervention, the coast guard on the Long Island side spotted the boat and rescued us by pulling Frank's boat into shore.

I remember the painful calls each of us had to make to our fathers at 8:00 p.m. to advise them that we were stuck at a coast guard station on the other side of the Sound and that they had to drive to pick us up. As the fathers arrived, Frank Herz's father announced, "You are done with the boat for the rest of the year, and maybe more." There was no resistance to Mr. Herz's statement, and we readied ourselves for a three-hour ride back to Mamaroneck in silence.

After we got back, my father had a conundrum, and it was time for him to take charge, again. "We came here from Chicago two years ago

12

because I got a big promotion in the office and a big raise that came out of it," he said at a Sunday night dinner in a calm voice. "A couple of you have liked living here," he said, looking at me and John, "and some of you were not so sure," he continued, looking at my sisters, "but there are mixed feelings, and there are some feelings that are not so mixed," he said, looking at all of us this time. My dad then looked at my mother, and it was clear that he had come to a conclusion with my mother about what he was going to say next.

My dad was always one to speak his mind, and when he did, it was with great conviction. None of my siblings tried to negotiate with my dad, because when they did, they always lost.

He continued, "Your mom misses Chicago and her friends there. She is stressed about it, and I am worried, so I have decided to do something about it." The kids all raised their eyebrows in unison. "I have decided to start my own company in Chicago, so I have quit my job here, and we are moving back."

CHAPTER 6

BACK TO CHICAGO

"BACK TO CHICAGO IN TWO weeks." There it was. The decision had been made by Dad, and it was back to Chicago for our family.

I was a bit conflicted about the whole thing. I loved Chicago and always felt best there, but I had made a lot of friends in Mamaroneck and was becoming fond of my recent girlfriend. Moreover, I had become a starter on the Mamaroneck JVs and a benchwarmer who got into games on the varsity football team, and to add to that, I had learned that the New Trier football team—which I would be returning to play on—ran a single-wing offense, which was much more complex than the T formation, which Mamaroneck was running and which was complicated to learn and hard to run. While I had enjoyed success at Mamaroneck, I would be scrambling for playing time if I went to New Trier.

So off to Chicago it was. We easily sold our home in Larchmont without a problem. The goodbyes in Mamaroneck were said, the moving van was packed, and away went the Byrums in their 1958 Chevy station wagon, all seven of us. I felt like I had come home when we drove over the big loops of the Chicago Skyway, then up the Dan Ryan Expressway and the Eden's Express, and then we saw Wilmette again after two years. We were really home.

We were moving to Winnetka. It was the town in which Greeley School was located, and it was the first school I had gone to after we had moved from our last apartment in Evanston. Our new home in Winnetka was located across the street from the Chicago & North Western commuter railroad tracks and had regular trains from the downtown northwestern section to the station in Winnetka. Once we moved back to Winnetka, my dad did not take the train between our home and his office downtown, as he had in Mamaroneck; instead, he chose to drive to the city each day.

Upon my return to the Cedar Street home in Winnetka, I was greeted by Chris Kruger, a classmate of mine at Avoca, and Mike Paul, a new classmate of mine at New Trier. Because I had gone to several schools in Wilmette and Winnetka by the time I enrolled at New Trier, I was joined there by many students who were already friends or associates, and I was quickly absorbed by many in the New Trier student body, without further introduction, and absorption into the high school was an easy matter.

CHAPTER 7

NEW TRIER

THE ENROLLMENT AT MAMARONECK HAD been 1,600 students in my last year there, while the enrollment at New Trier was over 4,000, leaving the New Trier students a very high likelihood to compete for everything, from grade point averages to sports teams. This made me nervous about competing at New Trier for playing time in football, or even making the team by going there, when things would have been easier had I stayed at Mamaroneck; but I'd had no choice. While making the team at New Trier was a situation I had to deal with, I also had a problem finding a position. The New Trier football coach for many years was the legendary Walter Aschenbach, who had earned his fame as a player at Dartmouth and went on to coach New Trier teams for forty years before retiring in 1965. Coach Aschenbach learned to coach his teams to run the single-wing offense, which I was not familiar with at Mamaroneck and had to learn from scratch at New Trier. I was put at the wingback position by the coaches because I was pretty fast. I played the wingback position on junior varsity, and another on varsity when I weighed only 144 pounds, not an ideal weight for football. My job at the position was to line up outside the end, where I could block, catch passes, and run reverses, which took some learning.

New Trier played in the Suburban League, a conference of the oldest and biggest schools in Illinois, and at the time, it was viewed as the premier conference in the state.

When I joined New Trier and was put at wingback, I was relieved to know that, although I was new at the position, I was going to be the starter my junior year on the JV team, and I played wingback for the whole season. The result was good for me because I had time to learn. I played a lot and would be ready for my senior year.

Coach Aschenbach reached a point in each season when he required every player—JV or varsity—to put a piece of tape on the front of his helmet with his name written on it with an indelible marker. This enabled the coach to remember our names. The exercise was fine because it helped get the coach familiar with his players and kept him in condition to teach the single wing and come up with plays when he needed them. It was a tough task for the coach.

The year that I arrived at New Trier, none of the coaches had seen me before. They had only seen the players who had played for New Trier in the two years I had played in New York, so I considered myself lucky that I became a starter for the JVs as a junior at New Trier.

The varsity team at New Trier was a good size and was plenty tough, and on every other Wednesday, they readied themselves for the weekend game by scrimmaging the JVs. Since we had our own practices and our own coaches, we were pretty much looked at as outliers to the varsity players, and they ignored us during the week, except when we scrimmaged them.

PLAYING AGAINST CHUCK MERCEIN

While there were a lot of good players on varsity, the best one by far was Chuck Mercein, who played linebacker and fullback for New Trier, and later played at Yale, and for several years, played in the National Football League. At 230 pounds, he was big, strong, and overpowering and gained a lot of yards for New Trier. Coach Aschenbach wanted to keep him sharp and effective, and the best way to do that was to scrimmage Mercein and the rest of the varsity players against that part of the team that offered no real challenge to varsity, and that was the JV players. The periodic scrimmages scheduled by the coach served this purpose, and the JV players knew it. The only way they would earn playing time was by making a good showing against varsity in the scrimmages, which lasted for about twenty minutes in order to keep varsity sharp and avoid unnecessary injuries.

On the Wednesday they chose to have the scrimmage, Aschenbach asked Peter Frandsen, the JV coach, to choose the eleven players who would be put on the defense for the scrimmage. I was chosen to play safety, a position far back from the line of scrimmage. This was good for me because most of the collisions took place with our line and linebackers, but it was bad if an offensive player broke through our line and linebackers, which would leave me exposed.

Our defensive team ran onto the practice field and assumed their positions before the first play from scrimmage was run. I sorted through my mind to make sure I remembered the three rules of tackling a big man because Mercein certainly was a big man, and we were going to have our chance to tackle him. First, rule: hit him low. There was no way a tackler could take down the behemoth by hitting him above the waist, where his bulk was locked. Second rule: keep your head up, and hit him with your shoulder but do not lead with your head. Third rule: once contact is made, put your arms around the backs of his legs, then drive him backward with your shoulder.

My plan to follow the rules suddenly evaporated when I saw the two linebackers in front of me scramble to get out of Mercein's way the minute he received the ball. Many runners would try to dodge the tacklers in front of them, but not Mercein. He was looking for defenders to run over, not to avoid. The two linebackers in front of me had not only scrambled to get out of his way, but they had actually dived to the ground before he got to them.

Suddenly, I looked up to where my defensive cohorts had been ahead of me and realized that I was the only defender left on the field—and that Mercein was not avoiding me, he was bearing down on me.

I didn't have to chase the big fallback to make the play, I had to prepare myself for when he collided with me. I just had to be in the position I wanted to be in when he hit me. All I had to do was crouch down with my knees bent, ready to spring at him when our bodies hit. And when he dipped his shoulder to make the collision that was coming, I sprung at him and hit him while he was lifting his knees to generate power. The blow came, and I felt like I was being hit by a truck. I thought I felt my brain rattle in my head as my shoulder and my helmet drove into his pumping knees. As his body drove me back, I reached as I was rolling to the ground and grabbed one of his ankles. As he stumbled downward, he could not regain his balance and found himself on the ground. My teeth rattled in the process when they took the impact, but none had loosened on me. It was over. He got up and ran slowly back to the huddle for the next play, and I checked for my body parts that had taken the brunt of the hit. A couple of my teammates, Mike Woloben and David Hathaway, ran over to me and helped me up. "Nice tackle; way to stick him," they told me. I think the whole team perked up by the tackle and gained some confidence from the event. It was kind of a David and Goliath experience, and it was worth the headache I had for the next couple of days.

I would do it all over because it showed me that I could play football against the toughest of opponents, and I would take that realization into every game I played after that one.

NEW TRIER VARSITY

My senior year at New Trier was a great one for me. For the first time in my football career, I not only made varsity, but I became the starter on offense and I even started a couple of games on defense. I immediately noticed the honor when I stepped inside New Trier High School. The nickname of the sports teams of New Trier was the Indians. This was a common name for sports teams in 1960, but it is now never seen because of the derogatory meaning the name conveys against Native Americans. The nickname of the mascot of the sports teams in any school, whatever it may be, is splashed on the clothing, windshield stickers, and book covers of nearly every student in the school, and the vocal support of the team is enormous at every game the team plays in, particularly in football. Such enthusiasm is universal in every sport, but it is especially seen in the sports of football and basketball played at the varsity level. This is not to say that enthusiasm and support does not exist at games involving underclassmen in sports like baseball and track, but it drops off in intensity.

I was very aware of this when my status as a varsity football player was achieved and I could wear my letter sweater with the letters "NT" emblazoned on it or my letter jacket given to varsity players to be worn in the winter months.

I played a lot of games at a position I was learning while in the process of playing, so I had a chance to start as a senior if things went right. My competition there was Rich Johnson, whose brother Frank had made all-state the year before for New Trier; but because I had better speed than Rich, I beat him out at wingback on offense, although he beat me out at halfback on defense, so both of us were happy. As a matter of fact, Rich and I went on to attend law school at Northwestern University and became good friends.

However, the hard fact was that I had never played with the varsity players at New Trier until I was a senior, but I finally got to do it and became a very good double-team blocker with our team captain, Tim Ade. While I fell in love with the game of football and turned out to have a pretty good career as a high school player, I never thought much about playing in college. This situation changed when Bill Fox (an offensive lineman who became a good friend after I secured my position on varsity) told me that he had an uncle who was on the swimming team at DePauw University. New Trier was a bigger high school (enrollment of 4,000) than Mamaroneck (1,600). I had realized this the moment I'd entered New Trier and saw the size of the school, which meant that its football teams had more athletes to pick from than Mamaroneck, which I also realized when I saw New Trier's football team. It was going to be more difficult for me to make the New Trier team, which I also realized when I saw the team. What's more, the opponents New Trier played were bigger and better than those Mamaroneck played, which also made it more difficult to play against the teams in New Trier's conference.

It was a slow growth process for me after my freshman year at Mamaroneck. I became a JV as a sophomore, and the next year, I would have easily moved to varsity, probably as a starter. But at New Trier, although my move was to JV, because I was an unknown commodity, I would have to wait until my senior year until I could make varsity.

I was happy to start at wingback for the JVs at New Trier, and then start for the varsity.

Playing a full schedule of games against varsity Suburban League teams was an honor and experience for me, and for the first time, I felt that I could play high school football at a level with the tough teams we would face in the coming year.

High school football is part of the American experience as middle schoolers move on from their experiences in elementary school and middle school and then to the next level of their education to the high school that will ready them for life in the workforce or in college. This experience is a new one for them and for those who continue with them, and it will be directed by their growth, both physical and mental. They are in a new place, which brings on new experiences, of which the game of football is a big part, as participants and as spectators. Their new place of education and subjects they study are vastly different from where they have been, and they are now Bulldogs or Pirates, rather than children in the grade school where they have been before.

CHAPTER 8

PONDERING COLLEGE FOOTBALL

Bill Fox's uncle suggested to him that Bill should consider visiting DePauw University in Greencastle, Indiana, while he was looking at colleges he might attend.

Bill was one of the biggest players on the New Trier football team, and he had received a letter from the DePauw football coach, inviting him to visit the school, which was very interested in having him attend. When Bill told me he had been invited for a one-day trip to visit the school, he asked me along to keep him company while he was driving back and forth from Greencastle. I accepted, and suddenly, I developed an interest in finding out more about DePauw University. My parents were happy for me to accompany Bill, as I had made no college plans at that point, so I made the trip to DePauw, which took about four hours to drive to Greencastle in Central Indiana, where DePauw is located.

At the time of the trip, all I had thought about was that: 1) I loved the game of football; 2) I would like to continue playing the game while I was in college; and 3) If I were to continue in college, I would like to know that I had a reasonable chance of making the team and getting into games. My dad was secure in his business and would be able to pay my college tuition and expenses, without the need for me to obtain an athletic scholarship. At 145 pounds, and with a high school grade point average of B, and without spending much serious time at the study table, I was interested in attending a smaller private school with athletic programs, so DePauw University seemed like a good fit.

Fox was about six feet two inches tall and weighed 220 pounds, so many football coaches had heard of him through recruiters and had sent him invitations to visit their campuses and meet their football coaches. He had the letters to prove it. On the other hand, I had yet to receive any recruiting letters for football from any schools or their coaches, so I had to tag along on Fox's trip in order to get a look at a program or talk to a coach.

We pulled into the campus at noon after a five-hour drive from Wilmette and drove around the campus on our own before our meeting with the coaches, which was scheduled for two o'clock. It was a beautiful setting with academic buildings, student dorms, and residential buildings bearing the Greek names for fraternities and sororities. Most of the buildings were old but beautifully architected. Students who were well-groomed and smartly dressed ran between the library and the various academic buildings. To Fox and to me, the male students looked much older than us, and very sophisticated. The female students were fashionably dressed in expensive clothes that appeared much superior than what was worn by the girls at New Trier, and they had looks of maturity in their well made-up faces and carefully coiffed hair. Although the girls were only a couple of years older than us, they made us feel like we were grade-school boys in comparison to the DePauw students. We were clearly intimidated and felt very out of place, but we were pleased to be there. We would remember them for a long time.

Our gawking was interrupted by our awareness that we needed to get to Bowman Gym to keep our appointment with the DePauw football coaches. It turned out to be a very important one to keep.

CHAPTER 9

MEETING WITH THE DEPAUW COACHES

AT TWO O'CLOCK ON THE button, we arrived at Bowman Gym, when Jim Loveless, DePauw's athletic director, had set up our meeting with the football coaches, Tommy Mont (the head coach) and Ted Katula (the first assistant on defense). We drove over to Bowman Gym where the athletic coaches for the school were located.

We had driven down in a black Cadillac owned by Fox's father, who let us use it for the trip. It was an imposing car and looked like it would be owned by a banker, a lawyer, or a mobster (take your choice), and the students on campus, most of whom did not have cars, took immediate notice when they saw the car.

We were ushered into the office of Coach Mont, who was waiting to talk to us. In front of him was a summary that had been prepared for him by a recruiter and a legal pad that had my name on it but nothing more. I was not offended or worried when I saw them.

It was no mystery who the coaches were interested in for the meeting. Fox was the perfect player for what the team needed: big, strong, and powerful. What's more, he was just smart enough. He could meet the challenges presented to the players at DePauw and could hold his own against them. He had been schooled enough by the New Trier coaches to talk about blocking and tackling, and by the time he stood up to leave, the coaches were all around him.

Coach Mont was a very impressive guy. He had been a star while he was a quarterback at Maryland and had been a very capable backup to Sammy Baugh when he played in the NFL. After his retirement as a player, he became the coach at Maryland for several years and even won an Orange Bowl game as Maryland's coach. He was very glib and was an excellent public speaker who loved by the press, but alas, his win/loss record turned out to be not so good, so eventually, he was released by Maryland.

DePauw had a good record with the coach after Maryland, and he served there as DePauw's coach, well-liked by school trustees playing strong schools and turning out successful students.

Coach Katula was an able assistant for Coach Mont. He had played defensive end at Ohio State University (OSU) in college and then continued on as a graduate assistant after he graduated from OSU. He was a tough coach and was admired by the players at OSU, and when his time was up, he took over as defensive coordinator under Coach Mont at DePauw. As a coaching duo, they were well-liked and successful. Coach Katula was deft as a scout and defensive play caller, and Coach Mont knew the ins and outs of offense.

I think that, in order to make me comfortable, Coach Mont brought us in at the same time for the interview, which was a smart move. Fox was clearly the player he wanted, but he was recruiting me as well. I would be playing in my freshman year, at least as a backup, but I might even develop as an important player, and DePauw would never reject a player who had played in a good high school and might work out for them, so the coaches kept the welcome mat out for me on this visit. Their decision would turn out well for me and the team.

Fox and I walked into our meeting with Coach Mont. He had already received our grade transcripts from our high school and the game films that had been given to him by our coach, and he had looked at them carefully. Fox's performance, as shown by the materials the coach had been given, were strong and positive. The materials also reflected well on my performance, particularly those highlighting my speed and my downfield blocking ability, so I took encouragement from the coach's evaluation.

The coach announced, "I know that you are aware of what DePauw has to offer as a school and as a football program." He continued, "You have decided to pay us a visit, based on what you have heard about us, and we like what we have seen about you. You are good students and are good athletes and should fit in.

"If you decide that you want to go here and are committed to put in the study time you'll need to succeed in academics here, you have an excellent chance to get the good grades needed for you to graduate. We think that, coupled with what we have heard and seen from your high school, you have the mental and physical skills to make it as a player in our conference."

Fox and I were delighted to hear what he had to say.

"I'll tell you what," he continued, "I want to give you some films from our game with Wabash last year. Wabash is our biggest rival, and our game with them is loaded with tradition. If you are impressed and you hit the books hard, you may have what it takes to be players here. The rest is up to you."

We liked what he had to say and called our high school coach in order to make arrangements to borrow his projector to look at the game film he had provided. On the way to the car, we stopped by the university bookstore to pick up a couple of DePauw Tigers hats, which we wore on the trip home. We also picked up from the coach a couple of copies of the program for the last Wabash game with the heights, weights, and pictures of last year's Tiger players. While we were pretty much sold on DePauw at that moment, we each had made arrangements to interview some other schools we had read about with small college football programs, and we went to look at them independently of each other, but each of us was committed. As it turned out, we would each choose to go to DePauw and play football over the next four years.

SELECTION OF A COLLEGE

When selecting a college, a player's first priority should be the quality of the education he will get there, whatever the size of the school. Secondly, he must be able to afford the cost, whether by obtaining a scholarship or digging into his own pocket or his father's. Third, he must love to play football. The question is, where will he play? If he is good enough to play at a big school, his talent should be extraordinary, and few are that talented.

Many players want the good education and want to play the game, so they choose to play in small colleges where they can afford to play and compete and can also obtain the quality education. They must love the game in order to do this, but they will be very gratified if they do, achieving their objectives in the process. They are not likely to play in prestigious bowl games, but they'll love what they do. This provides them with what they aspire to and satisfies their life objectives.

It worked for me. I was grateful, and it made a difference in my life.

CHAPTER 10

THE DEPAUW FRESHMAN TEAM CONVENES

JUST AFTER LABOR DAY OF my freshman year, I was driven to Greencastle by my parents to check in for classes at DePauw. Fox had been driven by his parents two weeks earlier to participate in early admission as an invited freshman player with the varsity team. I wanted to see how things were going for him with the varsity as an invited freshman.

I met up with him shortly after I arrived on campus and had been assigned to a host home on campus. Fox had also been assigned to a host home for rush but had been there a week earlier than me. Each of us had formed our preliminary opinions about the other freshmen we had seen on campus, and we were anxious to talk to each other about what we had seen, particularly the women, but that could wait. What we really wanted to talk about most were our new freshman teammates, some of whom Fox had spent the last week with in the football dorm.

We met at the cafeteria in the student union building at 8:00 a.m. as planned. This was a relief to Fox, who had been up at 6:00 and on the practice field at 7:00 each day of the last week because of practice but had been given the day off today.

"Well, what has it been like so far?" I asked. We had been teammates at New Trier and had already formed our own opinions about what the college team would be like, especially the varsity.

"They are big," said Fox, "and they don't just tackle you, they hit you hard, a lot harder than in high school." Fox went on to explain. "Remember that these guys are two and three years older than us and have been working out in the weight room for the last several years. They are like men."

"Well, they are men, actually," I said. "We've never played anyone older," I pointed out. Fox and I had played against high school juniors and seniors who were quite a bit different from the nineteen- to twenty-year-olds that Fox had just spent the week with. Fox didn't sound like he was afraid or concerned about the varsity players, but he took great care in describing them.

"Don't get me wrong! This is college, and the players take the game seriously, and that's how they play. You'll see." Fox continued, "Also, there are nine other freshmen besides me who have been practicing."

I replied, "Yeah, the guys who were the invited freshmen, unlike me." I sounded a bit resentful about what I perceived as a slight.

"How are they? We should be worried more about them than the varsity players. What are they like?" I asked.

Fox responded, "All good guys. They look like they are going to be good teammates. Mostly interior linemen, eight to be exact. The other two are Art O'Connor, a left-handed quarterback from Chicago, and Loeffler, a tackle from Chicago. Coach Mont likes the linemen because they are likely to be used in the scrimmages and drills, while backs are not, since they don't know the plays you'll have offered."

"Yeah, I guess so," I responded.

"Tomorrow you'll get a chance to meet all of them, varsity and freshman, so you will see for yourself."

I was getting pretty excited about the whole thing and the role played in the process by freshmen.

In 1962, freshmen could not play varsity and only played a freshman season of three games against other freshman teams in their conference. They still managed to practice every day with the varsity but were pretty much limited to drills and scrimmages, which were not very exciting.

The freshmen were scheduled to meet as a team that day at the meeting room at Bowman Gym, where they would meet each other. Mike Snavely, the freshman coach, walked out of the coaches offices to Blackstock Stadium and into the sunshine while carrying a Styrofoam cup of black coffee. He looked over the scene before him on the practice field. On the field, warming up under the direction of Coach Hosier (a graduate assistant who had been hired to assist Snavely in coaching the freshman team), were the twenty players he would be in charge of for the upcoming season. We had just started to stretch and exercise on the field and were starting to line up for some jumping jacks in unison.

The team had, from first approaches, a number of athletes who showed enough size, strength, and coordination on which to build a reasonable team. It also had a few members who showed absolutely no potential whatsoever and obviously had no reason to be out there. Fortunately, there were just a few of those, and the coach concluded that they would be out of there soon; but since he only had twenty players, he would give them every chance to disprove his initial assessment and to make the team.

As it turned out, only one of the players named Titzell was so lacking that he left after the first day of practice. Why he even tried out was a puzzlement. It had become clear when everyone was asked by the coach to name his preferred position, and Titzell responded, "Whatever," and was then invited to pick up his gear.

Of the nineteen remaining players, the five sizable linemen who had been invited to get there early—Fox, Terry Johnstone, Ed Gardner, Mark Moore, and Ralph Larson—were good players and knew what they were doing, so they were keepers, as they would be the offensive line and the defensive line for the varsity for the three seasons after freshmen year. A big quarterback from the Indianapolis area named Dave Joyce was a lock for the freshman team. A good receiver/back named Bill Coker and I would play the two halfback slots. (I had been a wingback in high school but the adjustment to halfback would not be that tough.) Two of the remaining spots to be filled were fallback, which would be manned by Tom Cooper (who played the position in high school in Indiana) and strong side end, which would be played by Todd Eberle of Missouri. All said, it had the makings of a pretty good offense. The same group would turn around and play defense, which was not a bad core out of a team with nineteen players.

Coach Snavely was well past his coaching prime when he took over the job of coaching the DePauw freshmen, but he had seen a lot of formations and had devised a lot of football plays over the years, and what's more, he had been placed in the role of having to take on the job of coaching freshman teams of all types with players who had not practiced or who came up learning no particular types of offense, so things were always a hodgepodge for the teams he took over to coach each year. He could bet that his teams every year would be comprised of players of many different football experiences who were products of diverse coaching systems with different playbooks. It was his job to assess the skills and experiences of each of his players, pick the offenses that were best suited for the team he was responsible for, and develop a series of plays within the system he chose so that they could become effective with every group. His decision was pretty much consistent with what he had done in the past for the unpredictable teams that were given to him, so he usually chose a system based in a straight T formation, with a quarterback who took a direct snap from center and handed off to a fullback who lined up behind the quarterback on one of the two halfbacks who were on either side of the fullback. The running players for the straight T formation were based on straight-ahead power-blocking by the guards and the tackles and sometimes were based on two of the linemen to cross-block defensive linemen across from one another. The straight T plays are like the ones that are run by high school freshman teams.

Once the straight T is mastered, the coach is able to sprinkle in some plays out of the winged T offense, where one of the ends spreads out a yard from the tackle he is paired with, and the halfback on his side lines up in the split between the end who has split out from the tackle. In that case, it is also common for the halfback to line up outside the end on his side where he can help the end block the man over him by double-teaming the man he blocks. The winged T crosses the possibilities of creating more running plays because the formation is at both ends and creates the possibility of running reverses and misdirection plays, making it harder for the defense to defend. It also makes it easier for the quarterback to throw and complete passes when there has been misdirection.

The DePauw freshmen worked for two weeks on running plays at passing plays from the straight T formation and the winged T formation, and we put together at pretty good arsenal for our upcoming initial game (one of the three we would play in our initial season), and we felt pretty good. We were beginning to play together as a team.

Two weeks before the opening game of the DePauw freshmen, Coach Snavely announced that the opening game would be played at Indiana State University in Terre Haute, Indiana, which was about forty-five minutes away by bus. There was some silence from the freshmen when the coach made his announcement because the DePauw players realized that Indiana State had a substantial number of freshman players who were recruited and were going out for spots created for freshmen playing football, and also that Indiana State had a roster of at least sixty varsity players that year and a freshman roster far bigger than the DePauw roster of nineteen freshman players. DePauw was in for a tough game.

The opening would be played on a weekday at the huge but ancient facility where Indiana State played its games. The DePauw team would suit up in its hand-me-down uniforms the varsity team had provided.

CHAPTER 11

POTATO MASHER

Soon after I arrived at the Phi Delta Theta house after pledging the fraternity, I was made to realize that, in order for the house to function and operate efficiently, it was necessary that the new pledges have certain realities and responsibilities laid out in front of them while they were there to upkeep and maintain the house and its assigned functions. The most important of these was related to the kitchen. I soon met the two ladies charged with the preparation of meals. These were Hayes and Cooksie, two women from town, both widowed, who supervised the pledges in their jobs of setting the dining room for lunch and dinner each day, serving the meals, and removing and cleaning the plates and the silver. That was my job for every other week at Phi Delta Theta. Both Cooksie and Hayes were advanced chain-smokers and could cuss with the best of them, and we learned to live with them.

On one particular week in October, I was assigned the job of mashing and serving the potatoes for dinner. I opened a potato masher and an accompanying cooking pot for every dinner, which included peeling the potatoes, boiling them, mashing them, adding milk and butter, and then putting them in serving bowls placed at the head of each table. Not a glamorous job, but a necessary one.

I had gone through my routine one night, when out of the corner of my eye, I spotted a mammoth moth with feathers that were almost bird-like. It came out of the corner of the kitchen and headed for the pot of freshly mashed potatoes, circling it for a landing into the middle of the pot. When the scene unfolded before me, I immediately notified Cooksie of the disaster. She responded with a few well-chosen cuss words as she saw that the moth was about to a nose-dive into the bowl containing the mashed potatoes. When she saw the moth disappear into the pot, she shrugged her shoulders, lit another Lucky Strike, and said to me, "Don't worry. He won't eat much, and it will only take one spoonful from the bowl for someone to notice what they have eaten." To my surprise, after dinner was over, no one had noticed they had eaten him.

CHAPTER 12

COLLEGE PLAYERS HIT HARD

I WAS ALL PUMPED UP FOR my first practice as a member of the freshman football team. The team was comprised of players from all over, with most of them coming from the states of Indiana, Illinois, Ohio, and Pennsylvania. There were twenty of them, and they were all happy to be there and were eager to show Coach Mike Snavely what they were made of.

Coach Snavely was in his early sixties and had been with the DePauw Athletic Department for at least thirty or forty years. He had always held some type of position with the DePauw football program as a coach. His experiences ranged from assistant coach for varsity, for the most part, to a five-year stretch as head coach (which, by the scores of the games DePauw had lost in the stretch, was not a particularly successful period in his coaching career). For the last ten years or so, he had served as the freshman coach. The only assistance he had was from a graduate coach, Tom Hosier, who had played for a small college in Missouri and was now getting his master's in physical education at DePauw and aspired to be a head coach someday.

Coach Snavely had no aspirations other than to run out the string and start to collect his pension, a process that would begin in a couple of years. He was tired, and it showed. He wasn't too animated or inspirational, and everyone knew it. The most excited he got was when someone made a mistake in his assignments in practice, which always resulted in Coach Snavely referring to them immediately as a "piss pot of cyst." By the end of the freshmen season, everyone had been called that name at least once by Coach Snavely, but some had experienced those words of encouragement five or six times.

During the first three days of practice, the coach went about the process of picking players for positions. The criteria he used were: 1) what position they played in high school, 2) where they had gone to high school (with the bigger, more prominent schools having the most credibility), 3) how big and/or fast they were, and 4) how hard they could hit on blocks and tackles. It was pretty easy to tell right away who the better ones were. The DePauw freshman team was blessed to have five interior linemen (Fox and four others: Ed Gardner, Ralph Larson, Terry Johnston, and Mark Moore) who had all played in good high school programs and who were all 230 pounds or so, which was a good size for small-college interior linemen in the 1960s. These five players all would go on to become building blocks for the DePauw team for the next four years, playing as a unit, except for Ralph Larson, who suffered a serious knee injury in his junior year that would shorten his career.

For the first four days of freshman practice, Coach Snavely concentrated on positioning players in offensive and defensive roles. There were two practices a day. The first went from 9:00 to 11:30 a.m., with a break of two hours for lunch and a rest, followed by another practice from 2:00 to 5:00 p.m. By the end of the fourth day, we could run about twenty of the basic offensive plays in the Tiger playbook. I had usurped the position of left halfback, and while it was a lot different than the position of a wingback in the single wing, which I had played in high school, it was not very hard to grasp.

During the first four days of practice, the team worked on lining up and running their blocking assignments on full-size tackling dummies or handheld blocking pads held by the defense players. They did not scrimmage. This would change on Friday, as Coach Mont walked over to the team and announced, "You freshmen have looked pretty good." The teammates all smiled. "Good enough to scrimmage the varsity tomorrow." The freshmen instinctively shouted out, "Yeah!" This was just what one would expect from a group of eighteen-year-old athletes brimming with testosterone.

"Good," retorted Coach Mont. "We will all take calisthenics together at nine o'clock and then start the scrimmage. This is what you came here for, to play varsity football against varsity players, so let's start you out with the best there is, the DePauw varsity."

"Yeah!" responded the freshmen enthusiastically and in unison.

I looked at the members of the varsity team to get a better look at the players, who we had not paid much attention to in the first four days of practice. The DePauw freshmen, in turn, looked at the approaching members of the varsity team, who looked bigger and older than anyone they had played with or against before in their lives. With natural growth and training, the varsity players were between ten and twenty pounds larger than their freshman counterparts.

The freshmen spent the evening (and for some, well into the night) with mixed emotions of excitement and apprehension about what would happen the next day.

The next day, as Coach Mont called the team up to the area where the scrimmage would take place, he explained that the ball would be put in play by the offensive team who had it, freshman or varsity, from the same spot for every play. This meant that if a team made a big gain on a play, the ball would still come back to the same starting point for the next ten plays. The freshmen would start out for ten offensive plays, then the varsity would take over for ten plays.

I got a little nervous at the thought of starting out with the ball in front of the whole football program—varsity, freshmen, and coaches—but I stepped into the huddle. Dave Joyce, the freshman quarterback from Richmond, Indiana, called the play. "Twenty-three on two," he said clearly and with the confidence one would want of his quarterback.

I gulped. Twenty-three meant the two back, which was the left halfback, would take a handoff from the quarterback at the three hole, which was between the left tackle at the left guard, then cut off of the block of the left tackle and turn up the field. While I was nervous, I was also comforted by the fact that Fox was the left tackle, and he had been opening a lot of holes for me over the last three years in high school, albeit from a different position.

I lined up five yards in the backfield behind the gap between Fox and Mark Moore. Joyce stepped up to the line and shouted over the audible. "Blue forty-two," he shouted to the left. "Blue forty-two," he shouted to the right. This enabled the quarterback to change the play if he didn't like what he saw on the defense or on the offense, and come up with a play better suited for the situation. Plays were changed when the quarterback thought they should be. It was his call. The thing to the audible as the color the quarterback shouted at the beginning. Red was the color he would show today if he were to change the play. Joyce has shouted "Blue," so the audible was a dummy call, and they would run the twenty-three. I would get the carry.

"Down, set," shouted Joyce. The offensive team moved from the positions with their weight forward and their right hands on the ground. They were ready to fire out. Joyce started the cadence. "Hut one." He had called for the play to be run on two so the team would fire out on their blocking assignments at the next hut, with the second one being hut two. Joyce continued. With the word hut, everyone did what they were supposed to. Fox would block the man to the left of him across the time to the left of Mark Moore who took the man across the line from him to the right. Ralph Larson would snap the ball into the hands of Joyce, which had been placed between the thighs and just below the buttocks of Ralph, and Joyce would take two steps to the left, parallel with the line, to jam the ball into my hands, as it had been called for me to take the handoff.

The ball was successfully handed off by Joyce, and I covered it with both arms immediately, like a back is taught to do, to avoid a fumble or to avoid having a defensive player poke it out of my grasp and recover the ball. I was now on the line of scrimmage, running through the hole Fox and Moore had so successfully opened, looking for which way to run with the ball, depending on where the linebacker and the defensive back were located. Suddenly, looming before me was the rapidly closing figure of Stu Young, the starting varsity linebacker for the Tigers. Closing in was the right team to use, because Young looked like a pit bull coming for a steak. Before I could recover, Young laid a shoulder pad into the number on my jersey with a stunning straight-on blow the likes of which I had never seen before, and it knocked me right on my backside with the ball still in my hands. I had been stopped.

Suddenly, I realized the difference between high school football and college football. In college, they hit you hard at every opportunity. In high school, they grab you and drag you or throw you down. In college, the force of the blow when you are hit knocks you down. I had played a lot of games in one of the better high school conferences in Chicago, but I had not been flat-out knocked down by the force of a defense player delivering such a blow as Young had. This was the way football was played in college, and I would have to get used to that. Every play would be like this in the future.

The next nine plays of the opening offensive series by the freshmen went the same way. The freshmen were able to fire off the line and deliver their blocks, but they couldn't sustain them, and not much yardage was made. I had two more carries in the series, one for no gain and one for a gain of about two yards; but on all carries, a significant physical blow or two was delivered to me in the process. The freshman defenses fared even worse with the varsity offense, opening gaping holes for their runners to burst through with ease. This went on for another forty-five minutes, and the longer it went on, the more beat-up and humiliated the freshmen became. Yes, the varsity players had the advantage of knowing the playbook and the offensive and defensive assignments much better than the freshmen, but even if the freshman had been able to study these things adequately before the scrimmage, the speed, strength, and viciousness of the plays by the varsity team could not be approached.

As Coach Mont blew his whistle and instructed the varsity and freshman players to return to their own sets of drills, the dispirited and thoroughly battered freshmen realized, to a man, what they had just been through, but also what they wanted to make of themselves in the future.

"Welcome to college football, boys," Coach Snavely shouted at us as we returned to our practice area on the field. Coach Hosier smirked, making no effort to hide his amusement at what he had just seen. The freshmen trudged off the field in a bewildered state, knowing that things would get better. They had to.

CHAPTER 13

THE CHUG DRILL

THE CHUG DRILL WAS NOT one that was enjoyed by the players. It was brutal and simple. Two tackling dummies were placed several yards apart. Two groups of players were lined up, one behind another, with the first two men in each group to lie on their backs, head-to-head on the ground, waiting for the coach to blow his whistle. When the whistle was heard, the two players jumped to their feet and charged toward each other. One of them was to run into the chest of the other, acting as a ball-carrier, trying to run through the other man before he could be tackled. The other man was to step forward and lead with his chest to stop the ball-carrier with his chest and drive him to the ground. The ball-carrier used his helmet and his shoulder while the tackler used his shoulders and chest. The key for each man was to hit the other hard, drive his legs, and overpower the other until one of them was knocked off his feet and driven into the ground. There was only a winner and a loser. There were no ties. A standoff or a stalemate was not permitted. Neither player could dodge or maneuver around a hard physical confrontation.

To be effective, the drill required the combatants to be of approximately equal size with no weight advantage to be given to either.

Knowing the chug drill was next on the agenda, I looked for groups with normal-size players, not some of the behemoths on the team, to participate with in the drill. I spotted a group of players who fit that description, and I scrambled over to join them.

My group consisted entirely of halfbacks, some offensive and some defensive. The average weight of the group was about 175 pounds. Coach Mont probably should have told the players to match up with a group of their own size when he'd announced the drill, but he didn't. It was probably because he enjoyed the looks of consternation, and sometimes panic, when a smaller player couldn't find a group of players his size. On this particular afternoon, John Barnett, a defensive halfback from Lebanon, Indiana, drew the short straw and wound up with a group containing some large linebackers. John didn't play in games much and was not expected to do so this year, when he would be a senior, but he stuck it out and planned to be on the team for the full four years he would be at the school. No one knew why he kept playing, but they respected him for the fact that he did. He rarely missed a practice, and he worked hard. He told everyone he would "wait for my time to play," and he did. But in the last year of his career, his time was running out. John weighed 170 pounds, but he was six feet tall (compared to my five feet and eight inches), and he did not have much body mass, giving him the appearance of a string bean. With great resignation, he lined up with the other members of his group and waited for the drill to start.

The way the drill worked was that two tackling dummies would be placed about one yard apart. Half of the players in a group stood in a single line, behind one another, seven yards behind the imaginary line between the dummies facing the players in the other half. This meant the first player of each group would look directly at the first player of the opposite group, with about ten yards between them. At the coach's instruction, the first players in each group would lie on their backs with their helmets pointed toward the gap between the two dummies. One of the players was given a football, one was not. There were several groups doing the drill, so when the two players on the ground heard Coach Mont blow his whistle, they jumped to their feet and charged each other, meeting on the line between the two dummies. Some decent momentum could be built up in ten yards, so when they met, there were some significant collisions.

It was the job of the man with the ball to run through the defender, not around him, while it was the job of the defender to stop the ball-carrier with his chest, then quickly wrap his arms around the carrier and wrestle him to the ground. The thing that made the drill so terrifying for the defender was that he had to use his chest to stop a player who had his helmet aimed right at his chest area, with a good head of steam behind him. It was designed to build character and toughness, but fortunately, it was only used a couple of times during the first week of summer practice and was rarely used at all after that, like on the Monday following a twenty-eight-point loss to Indiana State in my sophomore year when the coaches felt the need to infuse the team with some toughness that had been missing in the game.

After the first two players in each group went at it, the second two players faced each other, then the next two, then the next two, with the effect that each player and his counterpart found each other every time their turn came up. The players would alternate between ball-carrier and defender, to give each player the full benefit of the drill. Once you paired up with your counterpart, he would be the player you would face with each repetition. This permitted two players, once they were paired up, to work it out and understand how hard they would hit each other and where they would make contact. In my case, I was paired with Bobby Gardner, a tough senior safety from the Chicago Catholic League. Bobby approached the drill with the objective to put on a good show for the coaches but not get hurt or hurt his counterpart. Bobby was of the same school of thought, and the ferocity of the hits (or the lack thereof) reflected this. Most pairs of players took the same approach. The drill usually lasted twenty to thirty minutes, so there was a lot of repetition, and the two players who faced each other had to be in sync.

Early in the drill, I looked around at the pairings to see if there were any unusual size disparities. There were not, as I was pleased to see, but I did notice that John Barnett was paired with Bobby Gardner, who was a two-way player playing backup quarterback on offense and safety on defense. Bobby was 6 feet tall and weighed 210 pounds, which in 1964, was a pretty decent size for a player in those positions. He was in the Sigma Alpha Epsilon fraternity.

Bobby was a very serious and intense guy. Not only did he play football, he was also an economics major, so he spent a lot of time in class and in the library. He also waited tables at one of the sororities in return for his meals. While he was well-liked, he had boundaries you didn't want to cross, and every player knew it or suspected it. Suffice it to say, Bobby would not engage in any theatrics or shortcuts on the drill; he would go full tilt because that's the way he was.

About two rounds into the drill, the air was shattered by a bloodcurdling scream. Everyone looked over to see John Barnett flat on his back, clutching his chest and writhing in pain.

"Oh, my chest, my chest. I heard something crack. I can't breathe, I can't breathe." His voice was loaded with pain and panic. Everyone was stunned. Barnett was gasping for air.

Coach Mont came over to where Barnett lay, and he knelt down next to him. The trainer, Ralph Berlin, ran over as fast as he could and knelt down next to the coach. The two men had no idea what to do, and it showed. Barnett kept moaning, but he calmed down after about five minutes when he caught his breath, but it was clear he was in extreme pain.

Gardner stepped forward and said to Mont, "Coach, maybe I hit him too hard, and it was a direct blow to his chest with my helmet. I heard a big crack when it happened. I think his sternum is broken." This was a very clinical statement for a football player, but Gardner had minored in physical education and probably knew what he was talking about. As it turned out, he did. X-rays later showed that Barnett's sternum (also known as the breastbone, which connects the ribs at the shoulder) had, in fact, cracked as a result of the blow. No one knew this at the time, and the major thing the coaches wanted to do was to get Barnett off the field so that he could get the medical attention he needed and so that practice could resume. The players were clearly unsettled by the whole experience, and something had to be done.

Football players are trained to be tough, and Barnett was no exception. Not long after he calmed down, and after getting over the fearful event of losing his breath, he nodded his head when Coach Mont asked him if he felt up to having Coach Meyer, the quarterback coach, drive him to the hospital. Shortly thereafter, two players helped him to his feet and assisted him to Coach Meyer's station wagon that was in the parking lot. The rear two seats were lowered, and Barnett was laid out in the back area, attended by Ralph Berlin, and off they went to Putnam County General Hospital. Now, it seems in retrospect, to have been a risky decision, but in 1963, it was probably the best one. There were no cell phones then, and the hospital had only one ambulance, which may have been in use, so what was done probably got John to where he needed to be in the quickest manner.

Barnett was diagnosed and treated, and he went on to fully recover, but since he was a senior, his football days were over.

After Coach Meyer pulled out of the parking lot by the practice field, Coach Mont announced to the team that the morning practice was over, but to make up for the time lost by the incident, afternoon practice would start half an hour early that afternoon.

I walked back in the union building for lunch with Fox. For a while they were silent.

Finally, I spoke up. "That was pretty bad. I hope Barnett is alright."

Fox nodded. "He's alright. If he wasn't, he couldn't have walked to the car. He chose to play football, and he had to be ready for something like this to happen. It goes with the territory."

I didn't respond. I just shrugged my shoulders and started thinking about lunch.

CHAPTER 14

INDIANA STATE FRESHMAN GAME

AFTER LABOR DAY, THE FRESHMAN team started to practice on its own, breaking away from its role as practice dummy holders and scrimmage participants for the varsity players. That is not to say they weren't required to do those things anymore; they still were required to do both, but they also were able to convince Coach Snavely for some periods of practice to run their own offensive and defensive formations and drills. The number of players on the team was increased as the result of the additional players joining the team from the incoming freshman class. All of the new players had played in high school but had waited until the team was formed to decide whether they wanted to be part of it. Apparently, they liked what they saw and joined, bringing the number of freshman players up to twenty, and that's the number of players the team had to start its season at Indiana State. The equipment issued to the Tigers was not new and had been used in prior years. The DePauw freshman players dressed at Blackstock, hopped on the bus, and headed south on the forty-five-minute trip to Terre Haute to face off with Indiana State. The trip was kind of quiet for several reasons. First, the players had not participated against another team yet. They had been practicing the plays they learned for three weeks and had reached the point where they would execute their plays somewhat efficiently, running alternately from the straight T formation and the

45

winged T with a mixture of twenty running plays and ten pass plays but were not blocking, tackling, or hitting; they were just running through the plays without significant contact. Second, they had not included any sophisticated ball handling, a necessity for executing the plays. And third, they had not practiced to initiate and sustain their blocks or tackles as soon as the snap count. We relied on our quarterback, Dave Joyce. For all the forthcoming seasons, there was a feeling of apprehension that we couldn't do what we were supposed to do when the whistle blew.

The Tigers warmed up and exercised the way they were taught and ran a few plays without any contact. The referee asked Coach Snavely whether he wanted to play fifteen-minute quarters (which was customary) or twelve-minute quarters. DePauw had only twenty players, and Indiana State had four fall teams dressed for the contest, and its linemen outweighed DePauw's by about fifteen to twenty-five pounds per man.

The DePauw players and I were shocked when Coach Snavely, probably out of habit from the days when he had the varsity team, said, "We came here to play full quarters with a full game of four fifteen-minute quarters, and that is what we are going to do."

I was startled by the proclamation of the coach and wondered if I had heard it correctly. By looking at the startled faces of the other Tiger freshmen, I realized I had heard it right. To make things worse, Indiana State won the coin toss and elected to receive. They would show off their physical superiority right away, and they did just that.

DePauw lined up to kick off from the formation they were taught. The coach told the team to expect a return up the middle and to stay in their defensive lanes while covering the kick. Indiana State, however, called for a return to the right, which meant that each of their blockers picked out a DePauw player running down the field after the ball was kicked to hit the defenders from DePauw and drive them to the center of the field. This would open an alley on the right-hand side, which would be created as a result of their blocking the DePauw player to the middle and leaving Indiana State to clear on the right side. It worked like a charm, and the alley was so open that the Indiana State safety ran the ball back to the DePauw thirty-yard line. It took two plays from the point for Indiana State to run into the DePauw end, all with a successful point try. State was up by seven.

For the rest of the first half, Indiana State scored three more touchdowns, to none scored by the DePauw team. The score was twenty-eight to zero, and as the first half worked toward its ending, the twenty DePauw players regretted more and more that Coach Snavely had elected the game quarters would last for the regulation time of fifteen minutes. By the end of the first half, the Tigers were vanquished and were beaten up. It seemed that the time period from the end of the first half to the second half was only the duration of a heartbeat. There would be no rest breaks.

The eleven best athletes on the DePauw team were left out on the field to play both ways, including me.

During DePauw's first possession of the third quarter, we were running the straight T formation and were not making any gains. I had run two consecutive off-tackle plays in a row and was called to run a third. Every Indiana State player on the field was anticipating me running the ball and was headed toward the off-tackle hole and broke for the hole when the ball was snapped. At least five of them went right to the hole in the line toward me. Two of the linebackers hit me head-on with their shoulder pads and stood me up straight to make sure I wasn't going anywhere. A third player, probably an interior lineman, hit my right shoulder with full force and drove me into the ground. As I hit the ground, I felt a sharp pain in the area of my collarbone, which got even sharper as the player drove me harder into the surface. The pain was excruciating. As I would later find out, some of the ligaments between my clavicle and collarbone had been stretched and some has been torn.

The DePauw trainer, who accompanied the team, was not a doctor, but he had seen separated shoulders before. He knew that the best thing to do was to stabilize the shoulder to keep movement minimized, which he did with several layers of tape. Then he fashioned a sling for my right arm and put my arm in it after taking off my game jersey and shoulder pads. I then sat at the end of the team's beach and watched Indiana State pound DePauw with a few more scores so as to give them a final lead of forty-five to nothing.

After a painful bus ride home and an uncomfortable night's sleep, I set up an appointment with the DePauw Health Services doctor the next day and went to see him. The doctor agreed with the diagnosis of the team trainer and further immobilized the shoulder, telling me that I should see my personal physician. The only thing I could do was to keep it immobilized by tape applications and have it checked from time to time. Healing would take several months, and I was done with football until spring of the following year.

My mom set up an appointment with the family doctor, who was very attentive about meeting with my mother after the appointment. I got a ride home with one of my new fraternity brothers at Phi Delta Theta who was coming back for the weekend. DePauw was about a four-hour car ride from my home. My mother had not said much when I first arrived at home, but she told me she would reserve discussion about the injury until I had completed my visit with the doctor and had his report. My father had driven me to the appointment and was relieved to hear that the doctor's opinion was similar to that of the trainer. I would be idle for a couple of months while the shoulder healed but should be back at indoor practice in a few weeks, after my shoulder healed. My father was pleased that I was playing football in college. He had liked going to my high school games and looked forward to going to those that I would play in college. He knew that there was a risk of injury, but he was satisfied that I would heal and play again.

My mother had a different opinion about football that I needed to address with her after I got home from the doctor's office. She had always considered football senseless and violent, and she didn't want her kids to play because of the risk of injury. She thought that I would have grown up and given up football when I got to college, and she was more than miffed when I continued to play in college.

She was seated in the living room when I walked in with my father.

"So the doctor didn't tell you more than the trainer?" My mother grilled me I nodded.

"You were very lucky. You could have broken your neck." My mother had accepted the fact that I would play football in college when I'd announced it. I had played all the way through high school without serious injury, so she had reluctantly acquiesced when I'd announced that I intended to play in college. She now regretted that she had.

"How big was the player who hurt you?" she asked. "Bigger than who you faced in high school?"

I searched for the right answer. It was important that I had the right answer. My mother had always expressed her concern that I was playing against others who were bigger than me, putting all of my body at risk.

"Probably he was bigger than me," I responded, "but he was a linebacker, and they just tend to be bigger." It was not a good answer, and the expression on her face showed it.

"What did you expect to do, go all year without being tackled by a linebacker?"

"Well, this one was particularly big. Bigger than most," I offered. This was also not a satisfactory response.

She looked right at me, perhaps right through me. "This is college," she responded. "You are now playing with men, not with boys. The player who did this to you was no bigger than the other players you are bound to go up against in college. College is a place where you go to be educated for your life's work, not to get beat up and come home wrapped in bandages. You are there to study and learn, not to play football against a bunch of apes who work to hurt you and can do it. It is a waste of your valuable time and the resources of your dad and me to send you there. Don't you get it?"

"I hear you, Mom," I responded. "But football is very important to me. There are a lot of things I could do while I am there, primarily in the classroom, the library, and the study table, and I do them. I would only play football if I could budget the time I have to go to class and to prepare for exams first, and I do that. Please believe me," I pleaded my case. "Sure, I got hurt playing football, but I could get hurt walking around campus and stepping into a hole." I realized I had exceeded the realms of reality with what I'd just said. "Or something like that," I concluded.

All my mother could do was laugh at me, and she did, but she had calmed a bit. "OK. Let's see how you heal and whether you are cleared for spring practice. I am your mother, and my job is to prevent you from doing something stupid—and the job lasts forever. Got the picture?"

"Got it," I said. "Thanks, Mom," I continued as I gave her a hug.

CHAPTER 15

ENJOY IT WHILE YOU CAN

Playing football in my sophomore year was an exceptional experience for me. I made the varsity team. NCAA rules limited visiting teams to suit up only thirty-three players at away games, which made it difficult for coaches to coach. In college, most players specialize in playing either offense or defense. More skills are required for a player to play offense and defense in college than in high school, making it necessary for a player to pick one or the other. But since NCAA rules are limited to thirty-three players for a game, several players on each team are required to play both ways, spending their time on both offense and defense, or at least being prepared to do so. Because the grind of playing both offense and defense for a full game tires a player out and requires a lot of stamina, only a few players can do it for a team; and players who do must have lots of skills. Alcott was an example, playing fallback on offense and linebacker on defense every game, all season. Although he never got hurt, he lost at least twenty-five pounds over the course of a season, and he played relentlessly. Only a few players could do it. The players who played either offense or defense could rest when their skills were not required for the game. The players who played both ways could not. Unless a sophomore player was extremely good and was better at his position than the juniors and seniors who played his position, he had very limited playing time, and for the most part, he sat on the bench, waiting for his turn to play.

I was a good halfback and was fast, but as a sophomore, I was not better than the upperclassmen ahead of me, so most of my sophomore year was spent on the bench with the other sophomores. I only got into games when an upperclassman halfback unexpectedly got hurt, and only for the time it took for the injured player to recover, which usually did not take long. I also got into games at the end when DePauw was way ahead or way behind, during the "garbage time" it took for the game to end. I had recovered from the shoulder injury I had sustained in my freshmen year, so I loved the opportunities to get in the game when they came up.

Even if they did not all get into the game on Saturdays, when the whole team was announced and ran onto the field, the music blared and then the cheerleaders and pom-pom girls ran through with the chorus of the spectators singing the DePauw fight song. The bench players knew that they were extremely close to being one of the varsity starters at their position and that their time would soon come. They looked forward with eagerness to the times when they would hear Coach Mont or one of the other coaches calling their name and telling them who to go in for. Once this happened to a player, he would charge off the bench and run up to the coach, looking for his instructions while buckling his chinstrap. It was a moment I would savor forever. I was living my dream, suiting up for a varsity collegiate game and actually getting in to play, no matter whether it was for just a couple of plays or for the full three years of eligibility I had after the freshman season. This was an experience that only a small percentage of high school players went on to participate in, and it was not lost on me.

For the home games, I would usually sit with George Pierce, a quarterback from Kentucky, and Dan Brown, an end from Ohio. All three of us were players on offense, which pleased the coaches, since the coaches thought the players were all concentrating on their list of offensive plays and this is what they were talking about on the bench, which was not quite true. As a matter of fact, the discussion covered a lot of topics, not only football plays. The banter between the three of us ranged from the food at the union building, to the physical attributes of this year's freshman girls, to the quantity of each brand of beer it took to get a college boy drunk. They would have extended further if Bill Coker, who played split end with us on the freshman team, had been in on the conversation with the group. But Bill had quit football at the end of his freshman season and forsook college by signing up for the navy at the end of his freshman year; he was missed by his teammates. The three of us on the bench talked about football sometimes, while we were putting in our bench time, but usually it entailed our opinions about the abilities of the upperclassmen on the varsity team. Those opinions varied a lot, and I found it amazing how much time us three sophomores spent. I relished my time spent on the bench with Pierson and Brown, and I missed them when I accompanied the varsity team on the away games, as they did not make the traveling team. Instead, I often rode the bus with Denny Krutz, the equipment manager, with whom I often roomed at the team hotel for the away games. The upperclassmen usually talked between themselves for the away games and did not talk much with the sophomores. It was funny, but I soon realized that the approachability of the upperclassmen and their willingness to chat with the sophomore nonstarters had no relationship with the sophomores. You would expect the seniors on the team to be distant and aloof and the juniors to be open to conversations because they were only a year apart from the sophomores. But in many cases, the seniors enjoyed the opportunity to talk with the sophomores just to ease their nervousness about playing on the varsity team, and to give them encouragement and confidence about how they were doing. The same could be said for some of the juniors who were not starters but treated the sophomores with disdain, as if they themselves were all-Americans, but in fact, they didn't play a whole lot, at all. And sometimes not. *Go figure*, I would think. *It makes no sense at all.*

On the occasions when I did get into a game, my first priority was not to excel, but to keep away from making a penalty while I was in the game. No false starts, no offsides, no holding. If I could do this, I was a success. My big plays would all come later. I would be ready for them, and I was hungry for the opportunity.

CHAPTER 16

RECUPERATION
AFTER BALL STATE

The Sunday morning after the Ball State home game, I slept until nine o'clock and had a lot of trouble just getting out of bed. Everything ached, and I felt the effects of every hit I had given or received the day before against Ball State. They were not a slick or speedy team, but they were big and large and could punish you, even if you were prepared for it. They were nasty and mean, making other teams aware from the beginning that if they couldn't beat you, they could still beat you up. They had beat me up pretty good the day before.

Most of the time, after a game, I had a lot of trouble getting out of bed the next day, as did most of the Tiger players (and as did most college players who played the preceding day), but this day was particularly difficult for me. My neck, shoulders, arms, legs, and knees throbbed. I had to get out of bed to start my day and forced myself to do so. Sundays were the roughest days, and it took at least to Wednesday to get back to normalcy. *High school had not been like this*, I remembered.

After grabbing a couple of cups of coffee and scrambled eggs and toast in the kitchen, I showered and headed over to the library to work on my term paper that was due by the end of the week, and to complete my research which needed to be done that day. Everyone was at school to learn and graduate, football players included, and no one was cut any slack by the professors. At a small private school, football was an optional activity. The players didn't have to participate; they did it because they wanted to. This was generally looked at differently than playing at a large athletic scholarship school where the players on the team were there so they could get their education paid for. Those players were perceived, rightly or wrongly, as being sort of victims of the system. Without playing a revenue sport, many of the athletes in these schools would have no opportunity to further their education, while a good number of athletes at smaller private schools were intelligent enough to receive academic scholarships without playing a sport. They played because they wanted to, not because they had to. Hence, they did not get the same sort of emotional support, particularly if the team they were playing on was not doing very well. Being a varsity athlete, I was provided with the academic support at DePauw.

I made my way toward the library, taking care not to limp, wince, or show any sign that I had been beaten up. To do this would be to send all kinds of negative signals.

Before I went into the library, I eased myself gingerly onto one of the benches on the front porch of the building. It was a beautiful fall day. The sun was out, the trees were resplendent in their fall colors, and the temperature provided a crispness in the air. As I settled in for a few minutes before I entered the library, I took the scene in, realizing how lucky I really was in that particular moment in time. Where I was heading, I was enhancing my education, and I had been afforded a few moments to kick back in a perfect setting and just think about things. It was eleven in the morning, and there were very few students walking around campus. *Not a surprise*, I thought. College students, as a group, like to spend Sunday mornings sleeping late, or in some cases, have to do so because of the excesses of the previous evening. It was alright. This wouldn't last forever, so I should embrace it and enjoy it. Life and daily challenges were right on the horizon.

As I looked out over the campus, I spotted the lumbering figure of Fox approaching the library. I waved, and Fox broke into a grin, finding a seat at the other end of the bench occupied by me.

"How do you feel?" I asked.

"Not bad, considering," responded Fox.

"Those guys from Ball State hit pretty hard, but the outcome of the game was unsettled until the very end, so the intensity of play was a little stronger. We lost by one touchdown. I hated to do that," I continued. "Well, you linemen have it easier. You are only one yard from the guy you engage with when the play starts, so there is no real momentum when you collide. Backs, on the other hand, sometimes run for seven, ten, even more yards when they collide. Sometimes more than others can tell."

Fox rolled his eyes, as I knew he would. Contact with an onrushing 250-pound person took a toll, no matter where the starting person was at. I was aware of this as he spoke. Fox was as beat up as I was.

"Are you here for research on your term paper?" I asked. I knew Fox was, since we were both psychology majors and were both in the same class for which the paper was due. I figured that Fox was the only student in the class who was further behind in his research than I was. I was probably right.

"Yeah," responded Fox, "but I'm not sure how long I will be here today. I took a hit in my lower back yesterday that is killing me. Ordinarily, I wouldn't be here, but the paper is due by Friday, so I only have today and five more days to write it. I've got to change my ways."

"That's for sure," I shot back, "but do you really think you can? You've been this way for years."

"Nope," replied Fox. "It will always be last-minute for me, but that's when I do my best work. When the chapters are down and there's no time to spare. Put up or shut up." He was honest, and he knew himself.

A lot of people have neither quality, I thought. "Some people always do better in a crisis, while others need to plan and prepare way in advance in order to accomplish a task."

"Just know what you are and what you do best, and handle life's challenges from that vantage point," he said.

"Tell me, Fox, what do you think you will be in life when you get out of this place?" I was curious.

"Well," said Fox, after pausing for a thought, "I probably won't be a research scientist. Too much planning and reading, lots of complicated stuff. These are not my strong points."

True, I thought to myself.

"And my football skills won't help me much with life. A 235-pound man who enjoys colliding with others won't be a good professional player because the people you are up against there are 280 to 290 pounds." This was about the normal size for a pro player in 1964.

"About the only profession that can use these kinds of skills is a bouncer in a bar," Fox mused. "And that is a job where you make a lot of enemies and not much money. I've got some time to think about it, and I'm not married or planning on it soon, so we'll just see what happens. I'm not worried."

He isn't worried, and good for him, I thought. *He really is smart despite his approach to things, and he is certainly resourceful. No reason to worry about Fox. He will do fine.* I really felt the same way, but just not in the extreme manner that Fox showed. He knew he would leave DePauw with a good education and the life skills to pass on something of himself in the world someday. Unlike a lot of our classmates who had zeroed in on their intended profession or career and were now developing the knowledge and skills to excel in their choice, I was willing to wait for something to find me, or to come across something myself and reach it then, but not before. To do something early in life just because "early is better" is silly if you are not sure you like it. Sample the menu, then make your choice, not before then. I was right.

Fox and I said our goodbyes and went to different parts of the library so we wouldn't distract each other with further conversation. I read some reference research and took notes for a couple of hours, but then some of the hits I had taken on my neck and shoulders started to bother me, so I headed back to the Phi Delta Theta house to do a little more reading and watch the three-o'clock professional football game in the living room.

As I looked around the library on my way out, I looked for Fox, but he was nowhere to be found. *Probably asleep on a couch somewhere*, I thought. Anyway, I would see Fox tomorrow at practice around three in the afternoon. As with the other Mondays in the season, we would watch game films from Saturday's game and hear firsthand what Coach Mont thought of our performances. We had played a tough team admirably right up until the end and lost by only seven points, but we really had no idea how the coach would evaluate the team's performance. I hoped it would be positive.

CHAPTER 17

DAD'S DAY

DePauw had a tradition of featuring a Dad's Day game each year in the second half of October. It was a game where the fathers of all players on the football team were invited to be announced before the beginning of the game and to walk under the goalpost with their sons to reserved field chairs that had been set up along the sideline of the DePauw side of the field. On each chair a placard of the son's uniform number had been placed so the dad could find it and pin it on his shirt or coat where it would remain all game. The dads and the players loved it as it was a special event for the men who had signed some pretty big checks in order to put their sons through school, which, while it was excellent, was also very pricey. It was a very nice gesture.

Coach Mont did his part, greeting each dad with a handshake in the end zone before the dad walked under the goalpost with his son. The people in the stands could almost see the chest of each dad swell with pride as he went through the posts with his son.

My dad, Chuck, had started up a publishing company six years earlier. The experience had taken all of his time ever since he'd started and would continue to do so until he later sold it. He wrote the copy, arranged for the articles, sold the advertising, and arranged for the distribution pretty much by himself, so he had his hands full. The major publication was a magazine designed for doctors, focusing on office management and practice developments. Dad was tireless in his efforts and was having some good success. He made his money by selling advertising space to pharmaceutical companies that advertised drugs that could be prescribed by the doctors who received the magazine (which was free). Dad's skill was selling, which had been his career before he started the magazine. He was usually on the road from Sunday night through Friday night; traveling to call on pharmaceutical companies to place their ads. He was very successful at it, and in the six short years since he'd started, the revenues had quadrupled beyond his initial expectations. His objective was to sell the company for a nice profit by the time he was in his early sixties and then retire, which eventually would happen. A nice American success story.

Dad was born in 1920 and was not a great student, but he had great native intelligence and even better people skills. He had entered college upon graduation of high school and bounced around in parts of three years at three schools when World War II broke out, whereupon he enlisted in the Army Air Corps and served as a flight instructor until the war's end. By that time, he was married to his sweetheart, Barbara (who had given birth to me, their first child), and had started his sales career.

I was well aware of what Dad had done for me and the sacrifices he had to make to do so. He didn't blink about encouraging me to go to DePauw, which was not cheap by any means, or to juggle his finances while his company was still in its infancy, to put me through school. This was a huge deal to me and would make a big difference in my life.

While Dad enjoyed following my athletic career in high school and well into college, as well as the activities of his other four children (a boy and three girls), he worked and traveled and also spent his weekends working around the house on maintenance and improvements to make life better for his family. He tried as much as he could to go to my football and baseball games (the sports I played in high school), but he could only go to one or so games per month during a sport season, and those were limited to home games.

I was not bothered by my dad's inability to go to a lot of games. I knew Dad was busy providing for his family, and that was more than OK, for I knew life would have been vastly different for the whole family had Dad not worked so hard. I was always very excited to see Dad in the stands whenever he could attend my games, and it meant a lot to me, making me try all the harder to get the block, make the catch, run back the kickoff, or whatever it was I was doing to make my dad proud. It was a healthy bond between father and son, and it didn't need to be overtly discussed for us to realize it and cherish it.

Dad's Day in my junior year at DePauw was now the first college football game in which Dad had been able to see me play. He hadn't seen my games in my freshman year, as the freshman schedule consisted of only three games, all conducted in the middle of the week, and were not easily attended by a working father. And I played very little in my sophomore year, thereby making a four-and-a-half-hour trip from Winnette to Greencastle to see me sit on the bench and only get into a play or two (if any) an impractical experience. In this, my junior year, in which I was playing a lot and playing well, it was different. Dad was anxious to see me play, and I was anxious to have him there. Dad and Mom get up early on Saturday and drove down to Greencastle to see the game. With four kids at home and my younger brother, John, a seventeen-year-old high school senior left in charge of his sisters, they planned to return home right after taking in the game, since leaving school in change was at risk because of his frequent lapses in executing judgment.

The game experience started out a little rocky since I noticed that, as the introduction ceremony was starting, Dad was not at his selected place in line to meet me at the goalpost. I knew right away that Dad was probably in line to make a final trip to the men's room to pee, which he experienced frequently as a side effect of the drug he was taking to keep his blood pressure down. It wasn't Dad's fault, it was just nature at work, but when Dad had to go, he just went because waiting could be disastrous and embarrassing. When I saw that Dad had not found his way to his place in line by the time I was only two players away from being introduced by the loud speaker, I dropped out of the players' line and scampered over to the group of players whose dads had not been able to participate in the ceremony for one reason or another. It was a group of eight players, and I added in their number by joining them at the last minute.

Later, after the dads had been introduced and proceeded to their sideline seats and attached their sons' numbers on their backs, I spotted Dad, who was proudly wearing my number 22. Dad smiled at me and just snapped his shoulders as if to say, "What else did you expect? Stuff happens." I smiled, and Dad smiled back.

I went in to have a very good game. I ran a kickoff back for yards, caught two passes, and rushed for about fifty yards. A couple of times, the crowd gave a heavy applause for plays I had made, and I knew Dad had taken it in.

After the game, I showered and dressed quickly, and Iran out to the entrance to the stadium and hugged Mom and Dad, who were waiting there for me. They didn't have time to hang around and talk for long as they had to leave to get back home before anything unfortunate happened. They would be back home by ten. We chatted for a few minutes, and they told me how proud they were to see me doing well and how they would tell everyone at home about it. I could see the love in their eyes, and I could hear it in their voices; it affected me deeply. I was very thankful I had been able to do well in front of them, and I told them it meant a lot for me to be able to do it. They just smiled. Nothing needed to be said. Everyone just smiled and hugged.

I walked them back to their car and stood there as they left and worked their way toward Highway 231. I wiped a tear from my eye as it sunk in how the day had been and what it had meant to me and my parents, whom I loved very much. I turned and headed back toward the fraternity house with lots of thoughts of home on my mind. It had been a very big day in my life.

CHAPTER 18

THE POSTER

THE HANDS OF THE CLOCK finally moved to 6:00 a.m. I had watched them creep along since 4:30 with little snippets of sleep along the way. I wanted to be able to turn over and get a couple more hours, but it wasn't in the cards. six o'clock was an OK time to get up and think.

I was in the middle of putting together a contract for a big real estate deal I was working on for the law firm where I worked. It had all of the things a real estate lawyer thinks about when he puts a deal on paper. The objective was not to miss a thing. I had promised my biggest client that I would email a first draft by noon on Monday, and I had arranged for my assistant, Jean, to be in the office by 8:00 a.m. to create the document. All I had to do was finish it by Sunday night and I would be true to my word. It was now 8:15 on Saturday morning when I pulled my pants on and tucked in my shirt, so I was right on track.

I glanced over to the bed where Bonnie, my wife, was laying on her back with her hair spread over the pillow, peacefully breathing in a state of deep sleep, as she always had. I quietly crept out of the room, making no noise whatsoever. I was confident that had I not become a lawyer, I probably would have been a very good burglar.

I made my way through the living room and through the kitchen, then I flipped on the switch to the coffee maker I had filled last night and proceeded into the den where my papers were already spread out in several piles, all seeming perfectly organized and properly placed for me. Bonnie

61

had not looked at things that way and waited until I had gone to bed to get the mess cleared up and organized by the time I got up, announcing she was not going to allow the den to be turned into a recycling facility over the weekend.

The den was a perfect place to work, particularly in the early morning. There were picture windows on three sides overlooking a large lot containing mature oak trees and pine trees on the south and east sides and a large detention pond on the north side of our house, which contained a fair share of frogs, turtles, and crayfish during the summer. The pond was only four feet deep in its deepest part, so it didn't sustain any fish life. I wondered where the other aquatic life disappeared to in the winter, but they always showed up in the spring, which also brought sets of mallard ducks for short stays, and occasionally, Canadian geese, which I would promptly chase away whenever they landed; the dirty things.

This morning was beautiful. It was mid-May, and the trees in the yard had budded and sprouted with full, leafy splendor and already hid the view of neighboring houses. I was in my own green, lush universe with the early rays of the sun peeking through, hitting my yard. I could get one and a half to two hours in before Bonnie woke up. This would get me through the balance of the contract I was writing.

I just stood there for a couple of minutes, taking it in, then turned to go into the kitchen and get a cup of coffee (which by now would be brewed and ready) before sitting down to start my work. I took a step toward the kitchen when a ray of sun reflected off the glass face of the poster and caught my eye. The poster was hanging on the wall right next to the door that led to the kitchen, along with a few other sports pictures and one of my two material sources of pleasure: a restored jukebox that actually played a collection of vintage 45-r.p.m. records from the '50s, '60s, and '70s. I could listen to them for hours. The other material source of pleasure was the poster, which I was now standing in front of and looking at, flat-footed and in silence.

The poster was an old poster from my alma mater, DePauw University, with the schedule of games from the 1964 football season. It was the type that had been taped onto store windows and thumbtacked onto bulletin boards and in other public places to inform or remind people who and where the local college team was playing during the current football season.

In my case, the team was DePauw University, a Methodist school with an enrollment of about 2,400 located in the town of Greencastle in the middle of Indiana. The border of the poster contained photographs of game action, crowd interactions, and pictures of the stadium. The schedule showing the dates of upcoming games and the opponents and locations of the games for the season was in the center, emblazoned by a big golden *D*, which also contained individual photos of the team members who were seniors that year, as well as photos of a handful of juniors who were expected to play a lot. The end player and their position was printed below each picture. Located in the top part of the *D*, as it had been for almost fifty years, was my picture with "Charles Byram, Senior Halfback" written under it.

I had asked the owner of the barber shop where the schedule had been displayed for the 1965 season if I could have it after the season ended. Recognizing me from the picture, he said, "Sure. I'd be glad for you to have it. Take good care of it, and it will bring back memories forever." I thanked him profusely. The poster stayed in a drawer for about five years after I got married, but one day, I came home and the picture had been framed and was hanging on the wall. Bonnie knew what it meant to me and how it touched me.

I stood in place, for how long I don't know, and stared at the twelve faces of young men in their early twenties with closely cropped hair and coats and ties, putting on their toughest faces since, after all, this was a football picture, and I thought back to the time when it had been taken and all that had transpired since then. Maybe it was because it was early in the morning with no clutter on my mind and nothing to distract me, but whatever the reason, my thoughts about the poster and all it had come to mean to me had never been clearer, even after almost fifty-two years.

The poster depicted the seniors and juniors on the team, in their sport coats and ties and short haircuts, showing their tough-guy faces, filling in the *D* in the word "DePauw," and the cheerleaders shaking their pom-poms at the players and making them as cute as can be by flashing their smiles, and I wondered if they could still do that today, wherever they were.

CHAPTER 19

STATE DAY

John Newby, the president of the Phi Delta Theta house, made the announcement at the house chapter meeting on a Sunday night, when they usually took place. The members of the Phi Delta Theta house all pretty much felt the same way about their fraternity affiliation. They didn't take things to great extremes by wearing their fraternity pins or giving each other secret handshakes on campus, but they genuinely liked each other and got along well. The same couldn't be said for all of the fraternities on campus, so the Phi Delta Thetas were fortunate to have that going for them. They were all good guys, with a few exceptions, who were going through the college process and educating themselves for what they would become; but in the meantime, they were having a good time when opportunities presented themselves. *A good place to be at this time in my life*, I thought.

John Newby was just the way his name sounded. A handsome, well-dressed prelaw student who was highly respected on campus by students and faculty alike. He was also a genuine guy who liked to have a good time but never got carried away with the moment, like some of his brothers did. A perfect president and a perfect representative of the house. Everybody liked him, respected him, and listened to what he had to say, which could not be said of every brother in the house.

The chapter meeting was at seven o'clock that Sunday night, a time when everyone was back from dinner (which could have been anywhere, since the Phi Delta Thetas did not serve dinner on Sundays), and before the brothers hit the books for the two- or three-hour period before retiring to bed to rest up for the week ahead. About 75 percent of the brothers were in attendance, which was pretty good for a Sunday night.

The chapter room was a locked room just off the hallway leading to the basement of the house. The reason the room was locked remained a mystery to the pledges, who also lived in the house. It was kind of an unattainable place where people had to earn their admission. It was no great place and was kind of dank and drafty. It was not very well lit, either. There were about fifty folding chairs where the brothers could sit during meetings, which never lasted more than an hour. The meetings took place about once a month where the usual things were discussed: house rankings on academics and sports, rush, and any news of the university worth communicating to the students. The Phi Delta Thetas were well managed with most of the brothers paying their monthly dues on time. Like it was with most houses, the bills were sent each month to the parents, which was a smart thing to do. My parents were always on time with their payments. This made me proud and grateful because I knew my father had just started a new business, so things could be tight at times, and there were four more kids at home who were not cheap to raise. I was lucky, and I knew it.

After the Pledge of Allegiance and the opening prayer were delivered by big Ed Gardner, who was a divinity student destined to become a minister, John called the meeting to order. There was not much on the agenda, except for an announcement made by John about a big upcoming event planned by the presidents of all eight Phi Delta Theta chapters in the state of Indiana. The Phi Delta Thetas were going to resurrect State Day that year. The reactions of the brothers were mixed. State Day had been an annual event, usually celebrated in one of the downtown hotels in Indianapolis because of their convenient locations. It was a full-day event where all of the active members of each chapter were included and were expected to participate in the day's activities.

The last State Day had occurred ten years ago, so none of the current Phi Delta Thetas knew much about it other than what they had heard from guys who had gone to the school in years past and had talked about it (as well as other remembrances) when they'd visited the house on alumni weekend. They always spoke of it fondly.

The day was programmed out and consisted of a meet-and-greet breakfast followed by some speeches from the various chapter presidents on timely college topics. There would then be a singing competition from the choral groups of each chapter, each of which had one, followed by lunch and an hour off. The early afternoon would be occupied by a double-elimination basketball tournament between the chapters, which took place at nearby Butler University. This would be followed by some quiet time and preparation for a reception, then a dinner and dance at the hotel ballroom, which included a speech by a famous Phi Delta Theta alumnus, usually in the legal, political, or medical profession.

State Day had worked well for years, but as was the case with many events involving college-age participants, alcohol consumption worked its way into the process and had become a lot more prevalent. Part of State Day was spent in the hotel rooms some of the brothers had rented for the purposes of resting between events or changing their clothes for the next event. Since bringing a date to State Day was encouraged, if not expected, of all participants, rooms were also rented for allowing the dates to rest up and change, as well. As a result, a handful of rooms were available all day for rest opportunities and preparation for the dinner dance; the rooms were also used as places to enjoy a few drinks. Gradually, this led to attendance at the dinner dance by some overserved, inebriated couples whose behavior was less than regal. Several efforts were made to curtail or discontinue the drinking and resulting bad behavior, but it was a losing battle and the various chapters decided to suspend State Day long enough for them to put together an enforceable plan that would restore the event to the more proper one it had been in the past. The decision had been made ten years earlier, and there had been no State Days since then.

One of the goals of a college education is to give young people an opportunity to mature, gain judgment, and learn to make good decisions along the way. This also means that, unless someone has graduated from college, the aforementioned goals are not likely to be met and the miracles cannot and will not be made.

This is one way to explain the collective decision of the chapter presidents of the Phi Delta Theta houses in Indiana to resume State Day. If an idea is a bad one and constantly proves itself to earn a discontinuation of the idea for any period of time, that doesn't turn it into a good one. It's still bad. This truism was not lost on the young men who had determined that State Day, during the time it had served its penance, had straightened itself out and shed itself of all the bad practices and habits that had built up around it. They wanted to reimagine State Day as a new, improved version when it was resumed. These were the thoughts of noble young men as they planned for the first State Day in ten years.

I had been appointed rush chairman for the Phi Delta Thetas through my junior year. At DePauw, like at many small colleges, fraternities were allowed to rush incoming freshmen during their senior year in high school in order to pledge them before the onset of the next school year so they could move into the fraternity houses as soon as they arrived on campus. This was not some progressive social experiment, but an arrogance that existed out of need. There was only so much housing for students on campus, not enough for the incoming students, so the fraternities alleviated things by pledging incoming male students before they arrived on campus. The system worked and prevented a bad housing situation. Were mistakes sometimes made that resulted in backfire between the incoming freshmen and the fraternities who took them because there was not ample time for them to get to know each other? Yes. Was there a better way to do things? Probably, but no one had thought of it yet.

I was excited because I thought the idea of State Day was kind of neat and might be an attractive event that would invite freshmen to pledge Phi Delta Theta, but at the same time, I was worried because State Day had experienced some indiscretions and embarrassments in the past which might cause the Phi Delta Thetas to be suspended if they occurred now, and it could adversely affect the decision of the ten young men who were already in the incoming fall class to be Phi Delta Thetas. It was a good group, a mixture of scholars, athletes, and government-type kids who were socially adept.

I did not have a steady girl. I just didn't care because the time I spent studying and practicing for football, plus the time I devoted to fraternity stuff, didn't allow me to work on a relationship. DePauw was a little different than most schools on the subject of relationships between men and women students. Because it was a small school in a town that had little to offer socially, located in a rural part of the state, men and women students formed relationships that were more intense and regular at DePauw than they did at other schools. It was sort of what people expected if they were to date. This resulted in a significant manner of time input and ongoing attention between the couples who dated. It was fine, but it created the expectation among students that this was the kind of relationship they would get into if they were to date, so for people like me, who felt I was not ready at all for a commitment, it was a little difficult for me to get dates since I was not deemed to be "serious" enough for girls to date. The answer to this was to date freshman girls who had not yet designed this mindset after being in the school for a semester. They, in turn, began to look at us through the DePauw way, and Mack and his like were back on square one.

I had developed a pretty satisfactory relationship with Sally Stevens, a Kappa who was pretty and independent and was perfectly happy to go over on the occasions when I called—without expectations of anything serious or long-standing—and would drink a lot with me and make out to reasonably exciting levels. It was a good relationship for me, and Sally was fine with it. She readily accepted my invitation to be my date at State Day and told me she would look forward to it.

I agreed to get a room with my fraternity brothers Tim Garner, Jon Swarz, and George Marsh where they could have a few drinks during the day, change for the evening, and take one of the chartered buses back from Indianapolis to Greencastle at the end of the evening's festivities.

As in past years, the dinner and the dance would be held at the Claypool Hotel in downtown Indianapolis, an old, dignified, and reasonably affordable place.

While they've stood as well for the Phi Delta Thetas—who were represented by chapters at DePauw, Purdue, Butler, Indiana University, Franklin College, Hanover College, Wabash, Indiana State, Ball State, and Valparaiso—some of the brothers and their dates gave in to the temptation to retreat to their rooms to have a few drinks. I noticed this when Sally and I walked down the hall where most of the brothers had reserved rooms and heard loud chatter and laughing coming from virtually every room. These folks should all have been at the interfraternity sing or the basketball games or some of the educational sessions that were taking place, but they weren't. They were getting pickled in advance of the major events. I could tell by some of the loud voices and the high-pitched laughter that some were well on the way.

Sally and I were the first people to the room that had been rented by me and my three fraternity brothers, so we took the opportunity to have a drink and exchange a few pleasantries. After about half an hour, we were joined by my three brothers and their dates. Over the next hour we enjoyed ourselves over cocktails and some cheese and shrimp that Swarz brought. *The suave rascal*, I thought. We were having a great time.

Suddenly, Sally looked at her watch and exclaimed, "It's 6:00, and dinner starts at 6:30 sharp."

The scramble to get ready was on, so my brothers and I were kicked out of the room with the slacks, sport coats, and neckties we were to put on and worked our way to the bathroom near the lobby which was full of brothers who had the same activities with their dates, while Sally and the three other girls went about the business of getting dressed and primping for the night's festivities.

Sally and I made it to the main ballroom by seven o'clock, only half an hour late. We didn't feel awkward because quite a few people were arriving at the same time and the diners were only involved in the salad course.

I thought it a little funny that there were a number of empty tables toward the front of the room, where the speaker's lectern was located, while the tables in the back started to fill up, as if the people in the back did not really want to be seen. Then, as I looked more carefully at the situation, I realized that most of the folks in the back were in various stages of inebriation, ranging from mildly to really drunk. What's more, some of the tables in the far rear were occupied by groups where the males had stripped off their sport coats, ties, and shirts and were sitting bare-chested and enjoying themselves immensely.

The master of ceremonies introduced the clergyman (who had nervously arrived to the convocation earlier) and quickly introduced the keynote speaker, Roger Branigan, a former Phi Delta Theta from Indiana University who was running for governor. Branigan, the politician that he was, had a sense of what now going on, sized up the situation, gave a speech that lasted all of five minutes, wished everyone well, and then hurriedly picked up his notes for the longer speech he had intended to give before scrambling out the door, trying to get as far away from the Claypool as he could, knowing that the cork would pop eventually.

My group, who had settled at a table in back, sat back and looked with amusement at what was going on in front of them. Suddenly, a female voice shrieked, "My God, they are thrashing the carpeting in the lobby. Come look at this."

Half the room left their seats in the third-floor dining room and gathered around the railing to look down into the atrium housing the lobby on the first floor. I figured the other half of the room was too drunk to get out of their seats.

The people who looked down from the railing took in an incredible sight from the lobby two floors down. John Deere, a local farm equipment dealer, had loaned two hay thrashers to the local chamber of commerce which was promoting agriculture month throughout Indiana and had thought it would be a wonderful idea for the visitors to the hotel (who came from all parts of the country and from overseas) to get a look at some state-of-the-art farm equipment that was used in agricultural operations. As a result, the two thrashers were placed in strategic locations in the lobby that would show them off to visitors but would not interfere with the busy hall lobby activities, so the thrashers were off to either side of the room. A new piece of equipment must be tested once it comes off the line and must then be moved to and from the large rig before it moves into the showroom, so normally, a small amount of gasoline—just enough to be used in these minimal operations—is put in the tanks of the vehicles. The fact that the vehicles had gas led to the events that followed.

While a good number of the students who went to college in the state of Indiana were from metropolitan areas, a substantial number came from the rural parts of the state, as were the two freshman Phi Delta Thetas from Ball State who knew precisely how to operate the machines and had hopped on them, fired them up, and were now proceeding across the lobby, tearing up the carpet with the blades. The operators were obviously very intoxicated and excited with their performance, emitting yips and yahoos as they drove.

The crowd was so engrossed by the scene that no one saw the four policemen rapidly descending across the lobby and onto the moving machines, and at the last minute, violently dragging the drivers down to the floor and cuffing them then rapidly taking them to their next destination (wherever it may be) while holding the arms of the perpetrators, who had glazed, drunken looks on their faces.

From the balcony above, the crowd from the dining room, which had been cheering and applauding the drivers, now booed the police, who had interrupted the show. As the police exited with their prisoners in tow, and the lobby was cleared of bystanders by hotel security, the college crowd drifted off to their rented rooms since the dining room was now emptied and didn't have more alcohol, anyway.

My group figured we would do the same thing. The buses back to Greencastle were due to arrive in about an hour, and there was probably not a better way to spend that time than by having a drink or two while the brothers and their dates went about the business of gathering up their stuff for the trip home.

About half an hour later, the soiree was interrupted by a loud knock on the door. When we opened the door, we were confronted by a visibly agitated member of the Indianapolis Police Department who walked right into the room, looked around, and exclaimed, "It looks OK in here. We will let you go. Take your stuff and leave the hotel immediately. Your buses have been called and are outside now." He was so wrought up by the situation that I did not even think about crossing him.

"Yes, sir. Thanks. We will get out now," I responded. And that's just what we did.

As we descended from our rooms and exited onto Meridian Avenue, we saw it was blocked off to traffic, and we could make out two televisions, three chairs, and a table that had been tossed out of windows several floors up and crushed on the stairs.

"Some of the brothers had crossed the line," I muttered in a moment of understatement. "I think State Day has had it."

The buses rounded the corner and pulled up to the front door of the hotel. The DePauw brothers hurriedly boarded in order to get out of the chaos and to settle in for the trip back to the safety of the DePauw campus.

As it turned out, we learned the next day that, when some of the furniture had been tossed out the window and onto Meridian Avenue, the police had responded by sending about twenty officers to the neighborhood in addition to the four who had remained after putting the carpet-thrasher riders into to paddy wagon for transport to the holding cells at the Indianapolis Jail. When the officers had arrived, they split up and prepared a room-to-room search. For the rooms where the occupants were guilty of nothing more than having too much to drink, the students were kicked out and told to board their buses, just as my group had been. For other groups in rooms where furniture was messy or trashed, or where moral turpitude had been going on, the occupants were arrested and placed in a paddy wagon for the trip to jail.

As it turned out, the two brothers and their dates were among those who had been arrested and had to make telephone calls to their parents in the middle of the night from the jail. No one ever found out why they had been arrested, and that was fine. Everyone figured they deserved their dignity.

The campus administration decided not to take any action against the Phi Delta Thetas or their dates probably because no one had committed a crime, and probably because a large number of students had been involved in the affair without any real evidence, and the conclusion had been reached that no outcome of an investigation would justify the expense, time, and embarrassment it would take to conduct one. I was happy with this, but I was still very worried about how State Day would affect spring rush.

My worries about rush were soon answered. Within two days after the story broke in the national newspapers as an example about the tawdry behavior that young people (particularly those who had come from privilege) were capable of, two pledges submitted their resignations, citing that not only were they expressing their personal displeasure of the Phi Delta Thetas, but also that their decisions were supported by their parents and their clergymen; but strangely, for the rest of the week, there were no resignations from the other eight pledges who had committed or the ten incoming freshmen. An offense had been made, but why had they not responded? I was relieved with this, but the next week, I was made ecstatic about the fact that five more incoming students to whom offers had been made accepted the offers and expressed their excitement about being Phil Delta Thetas. *What has this world come to?* I thought to myself that I would accept the situation as we drove back to Greencastle.

CHAPTER 20

ILLINOIS WESLEYAN

THE FIRST GAME OF THE 1964 season for the Tigers was against Illinois Wesleyan University, a small, church-related private school of about 2,500 students, the same size as DePauw. It was a nonconference game, so the athletic department had made very sure it had lined up a game with a team against which the Tigers were at least on even footing. Illinois Wesleyan was such an opponent. It would have been nice to have played a smaller school with a team the Tigers were likely to beat, particularly at the start of the season, but the fact was, very few schools that played collegiate football were smaller than DePauw, so the Tigers were fortunate to be able to find an opponent with roughly the same number of players who were the same size as their own players and had the same skills as the Tigers.

In 1963, the Tiger football program was in its eightieth year of existence, which was quite remarkable. The school was committed to intercollegiate sports, particularly football, and spent what was needed annually to equip the football team. While the conferences DePauw had played in over the years had changed, the opponents were, for the most part, from the states of Illinois, Indiana, Ohio, Kentucky, and Michigan and were a mix of private and state schools. A quick look at the archives revealed that while DePauw's football teams had, on occasion, played the likes of the Indiana Medics, Moore's Hill, the naval radio training school, the Noblesville Athletic Club and a couple of flight schools and had won handily, they had also played big schools like Purdue, Notre Dame,

Michigan State, and Ohio State, some on multiple occasions, and almost always in a losing cause, although they had beaten Michigan State once and Purdue once, long ago. Their most frequent rival was Wabash College, a private all-male school in Crawfordsville, thirty miles from the DePauw campus. The football rivalry between DePauw and Wabash was long-standing and fierce. Since the teams first played each other in 1890, they have played the last game of every fall since then (save 1897–1899, 1902, and 1903), and the series is recognized as the longest ongoing collegiate rivalry west of the Allegheny Mountains.

In 1963, DePauw was a member of the Indiana Collegiate Conference, which was comprised of most of the football-playing schools in the state of Indiana except Notre Dame, Purdue, and Indiana University. In addition to DePauw, the conference included big schools like Ball State and Indiana State; medium-size schools like Evansville, Valparaiso, and Butler; and smaller schools like St. Joseph's College. All of the conference schools were no more than a three-hour bus trip away, and the scheduled nonconference games could also be reached by bus.

The Tigers had played Illinois Wesleyan the prior year, at their campus in Bloomington, Illinois, and after a tight first half, had let the game get out of reach largely because a large number of complex passes were thrown to Wesleyan's Denny Matthews, a small but quick wide receiver. Most of Matthews's receptions were made at the expense of Ted Crouch, the DePauw defensive cornerback who was a punishing tackler but lacked the foot speed and reactions of Matthews, who was the superior athlete that day. I hardly played as a sophomore the prior year but I had a full opportunity to observe the unraveling of the crowd from my seat on the bench, and I could feel the frustration and anger seething from Crouch during the experience. He was humiliated. Crouch had a mean streak and was extremely strong as a result of his numerous trips to the weight room, which he made more frequently and more regularly than any player on the team. So, after the gun sounded to end the game, the Tiger players stayed clear of him as he showered, dressed, get on the bus, and rode back to Greencastle in silence. Nobody knew what was going through his mind, and nobody asked.

Things changed for Crouch after the game, and not for the better. As a result of being shown up by Matthews, the Illinois Wesleyan receiver, the Tiger coaches concluded that Crouch did not have the foot speed or reaction time necessary to be a starting defensive back, and from that point on in his junior year and into his senior year, he was the fifth defensive back, getting into games only when it was an obvious passing situation for the other team so that a linebacker would be replaced by a quicker defensive back to help protect against the passing game. When he did get into games, Crouch tackled the ball-carrier and press-pass catchers with a vengeance, always hitting them with a full head of steam so as to knock the ball loose or at least give them a headache. I thought that Crouch was too aggressive and presented the risk of missing a tackle than he could make, if he played under contracts, but might not make it he concentrated on just to the ball so quick that he could give a hard hit. But, as I noted, when Crouch hit someone, they went down and often stayed down for a while.

Rick Jordan had replaced Crouch as a starting defensive halfback for the 1963 season. Jordan was a sophomore and was a lot faster than the senior, Crouch. Just like in the year before, the game was played hard and the players were very cautious not to make a mistake that would turn the back over. I was the kick and punt returner for DePauw and carefully locked each ball I fielded into my hands and made sure I covered the points of the ball with my hands when I started to run, so as not to lose my grip. Whenever I felt the first contact as I was running, I covered the ball with both hands for added protection against fumbles.

Midway during the third quarter, Matthews ran an out-and-up pattern against Jordan where he broke toward the sideline; or, if a pass was thrown to him, he broke back up and fled when Jordan reached the first break toward the sidelines. The play covered sixty yards and was over just like that. This took the wind out of the sails of the DePauw team, and the next two possessions by Wesleyan resulted in touchdown passes on Jordan, each over thirty yards.

Coach Mont was visibly flustered and inserted Crouch as the fifth defensive back the next time Wesleyan got the ball, because everyone knew they would pass, and he had to stop the bleeding.

The first play of Wesleyan after Crouch was inserted was a little hitch pass thrown to Matthews at the line of scrimmage. The objective was for all the other Wesleyan receivers to run downfield and take the DePauw defensive back with them, leaving Matthews with the ball on the line of scrimmage with no defender within twenty yards. It was a smart play, but Jordan, a premed major and a straight-A student, did not bite. He hit Matthews in the shoulder pads and wrapped his arms around him to wrestle him to the ground. Matthews, being the competitor that he was, refused to go down and tried to fight out of the tackle. This turned out to be a major mistake for Matthews because, as soon as Crouch saw Jordan and Matthews start each other up, he made a beeline, and when he was above three yards from the two players, he lowered his head and his right shoulder, taking aim at Matthews's lower left leg. The sound of the loud crack when Crouch's shoulder hit Matthews's chin because the knee and foot were unmistakable. A bone had been broken. To his credit, Matthews did not cry out when he went down, but it was clear by the amount of writhing that went on after he hit the ground that he was in great pain. It turned out to be a severely fractured ankle, and after the injury cart came out and took him to the waiting ambulance that was always at games for moments like this, Matthews's teammates knew he was gone, not only for the rest of the day, but also for the year.

While the ministering of Matthews was going on, Crouch, who had gotten to his feet after making the tackle, hit his shoulder pads, first the left one, then the right one, with the opposite hand, a mannerism he had adopted over the years whenever he made a big hit. It was his way of saying with his body, "I did in this once, and I'm ready to do it again." This did not surprise or offend anyone. Heck, it was common for football players to acknowledge or celebrate big hits like the one he had just delivered, even if the result was an injury to a player (just like it was here), but I become a little unsettled when I saw Crouch's mouth turn into a smirk. I could read Crouch's thoughts as I looked into his eyes. "I've waited a year for this, you little show-off son of a bitch. You shaved me up and humiliated me, and this is the payback. How do you like it?"

Like anything else in life, I thought, *there are unexpected consequences for our actions. It's a good idea to try to analyze them and look out for them.*

The final gun signifying the end of the game went off. DePauw had opened its season with a home loss.

CHAPTER 21

THE SMALL-COLLEGE
FOOTBALL COACH

OF ALL PROFESSIONS, BEING A head football coach is one of the most intriguing, and coaching at a small college where most of the players are not dependent on an athletic scholarship to pay for their education is even more so. In football, where most coaches are former players, it is always remarkable that so many men whose involvement in the game of football at the playing field consisted of learning and executing the plays that were in the team playbook develop and process the skills that are necessary for success as a coach, without any formal training.

A head coach is a gambler and a risk-taker. His livelihood is dependent upon putting in everything he has, to be washed up on the line each Saturday afternoon. He either wins or he loses in front of a stadium full of people who have put so much of their lives on the outcomes of the games they watch. There is no middle ground. The teacher deals in the abstract and strives to provide for young people a sense of inquisitiveness and the ability to analyze; they lead but are not expected to and do not provide definitive answers to the questions that come up while they teach or to be precise in his answers, or to be accountable, On the other hand, the football coach wins or loses each week while being compared against an equally talented counterpart on the other side of the field who has been vetted by the hiring process and has recruited the players and formulated the plays that are best suited to bring a victory to the school that employs him. By the time a coach has reached the college level, his coaching opponents are (if high schools have done their homework) every bit as intelligent, resourceful, and inspirational as he is; yet, every week, for every coach who wins a game, there is another coach who has lost it.

Sometimes a coach will be given the time he really needs to develop a program and will have the time to asses and recruit the talents he needs in order to develop the relationships with high school coaches and the education necessary to establishes pipelines into his program and to compile a win/loss record that will provide a little cushion for him if he sometimes has a down year; but more often, he is not given the luxury. If a coach is not a proven, reliable winner with his program within five years after he is hired, he is in trouble and will likely be gone. So why do so many want to do it?

First, there is the money. A good college head football coach is usually the most highly compensated employee of the school where he works, by a long shot. He will make an amount that is at least equal to (and, in some cases, more than) the salaries of the president and the department heads of the school, and he will have signed a multiyear contract to continue the process. He will also generate a second layer of income from his endorsements for athletic products and speaking for whatever he is paid to talk to a group about. In addition to the financial benefits, he will have power and adulation from the general public, second only to rock stars and movie stars (and way ahead of politicians). However, as in any business with high risk and high reward, failure of any type can derail a career with very little chance of recovery, but no coach who has successfully risen through the ranks will ever envision failure or even the possibility of it until it happens.

Successful football coaches in big-time schools are only expected to do two things themselves: recruit and win. And they have a lot of highly paid assistants to help them do just that. While the school has also put together the legions of other personnel to help a program to succeed—the trainers the tutors, the psychologists, the social workers, the nutritionists, and the career advisers, just to name a few—the head coach doesn't get involved much, if at all. He has confidence that everything has been provided by the school. All he has to do is win and keep the stadiums full for as long as he can. The number of men who can do that on a sustained basis without cheating is very small. This is why they are paid so much.

But what about head coaches at small colleges? They don't have nearly the budgets or the resources that the big schools have. For starters, in 1964 when I played, small colleges didn't offer athletic scholarships because they didn't have the resources to do so. Moreover, the blue-chip prospects didn't want to go to small colleges that were likely to lose to larger, superior opponents, thereby diminishing their chance to excel personally, so it just didn't happen. Sometimes a great athlete would also have the academic ability to qualify for an academic scholarship at a small school and would achieve the financial support he needed for his education along the way, but it was rare. Therefore, the talent pool that a small-college coach could draw on was not full of skilled kids who could get athletic scholarships, and as a result, the players on the team would be volunteers who played for the sheer love of playing and for no other reason, monetary or otherwise. This added a new vital dimension to how he would structure and operate his programs, and it would be done by him personally (or with whatever support the school could provide to him) and not by members of some deeply layered staff.

The task in front of a small-college coach is daunting. He has to actively recruit from the applications the school has received, and in some cases, he must identify the players he wants to recruit and convince them to apply. He must monitor the applications through the administration office, exerting whatever influence he can (which oftentimes is not much in a small school) and must explore other sources of scholarship money or athletic jobs for the recruits that need financial aid. Once his recruits are accepted, he must continue to convince them to come to his school rather than one of the other schools the kid has applied to. The athletic department's phone bill can be staggering during this period.

Once his recruiting class has arrived, he is a surrogate parent to a group of youngsters who probably have not been away from home for an extended period of time and are now faced with the prospect of settling in for a four-year stay to prepare for life after college; and they recognize, sometimes for the first time, that their simple childhoods are over. Substantial experience in psychology is a very helpful thing for a coach to have; but typically, he doesn't have it, so he has to wing it. Helping his new recruits through their adjustments also includes intervening with members of the faculty whose courses, teaching skills, or expectations are in conflict with what the new recruits need, want, or expect themselves. Often, there is inflexibility here, especially when a faculty member doesn't want it thought that he is "helping out" a football player. Finally, there is a level of surrogate parenting he provides generally to the new recruits for the ordeals they experience upon arrival and throughout their stay in college. In some cases this extends to career planning and advice on what to expect after college. The coach is on the field with them two or three hours a day and is probably the adult they have the most interaction with, so by default, he is in loco parentis with anything that comes up for which a parent is needed but cannot be there. With a group of recruits, these tasks can convince throughout as full four years they are there. Multiply this by four because he is performing these tasks for kids in the freshman, sophomore, junior, and senior classes.

All of this takes place before any attention to learning the plays, attending practices, and game-day responsibilities that the recruits rely on the coach for. The thought of all of this, and the experiences of the coaches who go through it without help, is overwhelming, but if you ask any small-college head coach, he will tell you this is what he'd bargained for, and it's what he loves about the job—and he will have been truthful.

Fortunately, small-college players rarely become professional players, so the coaches are spared from that ordeal. If a coach annually turns out a group of intelligent kids who are focused on developing a set of personal goals and reaching them with the help and direction of the coach along the way, and ultimately providing for their families, he has done his job.

CHAPTER 22

HANGING OUT WITH PHI DELTA THETA PLAYERS

AFTER THE CONCLUSION OF THE Ball State game, I limped to the fraternity house with the other three fraternity brothers who had experienced playing time in the game. There was Stu Young, a senior premed major who was a tenacious linebacker who never played much before his senior year but had picked up enough weight and showed enough playing intelligence in the spring practice and preseason summer practice that the coaches saw fit to make him a starter. It turned out to be a good decision. There was also Bill Alcott from Youngstown, Ohio, who was another premed major who played two ways, as a fullback on offensive and as a linebacker on defense, both as a starter. He was a very quiet, guarded person on the football field, in the fraternity house, and everywhere else. Everyone respected Alcott so they give him his space. The third player was Ed Gardner, a junior like me, but a big specimen, even in 1963. Ed was an offensive tackle who was about six feet three inches tall and weighed about 240 pounds, all of it muscle. Ed was quick and strong and was the best offensive lineman on the team. I often wondered why Ed had not played on a more competitive football team. He easily could have eventually figured out that he, being a very religious individual with aspirations of being a minister, had found

DePauw to be the perfect environment for him and for what he wanted to do with his life. He was an only child, and his parents looked at things the same way he did. They could afford to send him to DePauw, so they did. Although Ed had higher ambitions in life than football, he was very good at it and could knock an opposing lineman flat on his back. Everyone on the team was glad he was there. Ed was very intelligent and philosophical about life, which sometime could be more intimidating to people who knew him because of his size.

For the first time since I had started playing in college, I felt like I belonged. I was now the primary kick and punt returner and was frequently put in as receiver on offensive plays. I added value to the team now because I would have an impact on how the game turned out. Last year, I had been a team member and traveled with the rest of the squad for all games, but I played only in spot situations when the team was way ahead (rarely) or way behind (more often). Nonetheless, I loved being a part of the team and being a football player, so I did it; however, I probably would have stopped by my junior year if my stock hadn't risen, but it did rise, so I loved it all the more.

My freshman year had been a lost cause because I had severely separated a shoulder while being tackled in the Indiana State game (one of the three games the freshman team would play), and I was out all year due to that injury. My sophomore year was spent on the bench. I had started to ache from the games after I showered and dressed. The adrenaline that was released into my body by my system was now gone, and some of the severe hits I had received or delivered during the games were now starting to make themselves felt. It would get worse at night.

I didn't hang out with Young or Alcott much, even though they lived in the same fraternity house. They were seniors and premed majors to boot, which meant they studied a lot more than I did as a psychology major. Although I hung out with Ed Gardner more, as we were both juniors and went to a lot of classes together, Ed and I really had entirely different interests, and although we saw each other a lot, we didn't converse much. For a while, at least, the 1964 season would bring us all together more, even if it was only for the season. None of us had any football expectations beyond college. Young and Alcott wanted to go to med school and go on to become doctors (which they did), and Ed Gardner wanted to become a minister (which he did). I, on the other hand, had no idea what I wanted or what I would do after college. *Maybe being with guys who had direction would help,* I thought.

The Phi Delta Theta house was about a twenty-minute walk from the stadium. All four players were still reliving the Illinois Wesleyan game in their minds and pondering the things that did or did not happen that had affected the outcome, so we didn't talk much at all.

Playing football is a lot different than playing other sports. Whereas all sports (including football) require speed, dexterity, endurance, and strength in different degrees, and a lot of talent in order to be played at the college level, football is also a game of brutality. In addition to other athletic skills, it requires the ability and willingness to unload on an opponent and knock him to the ground with as much force as a player can muster. It is not new or out of character for college players. They have been doing it for around ten years by this time in their careers, and by the time they reach college, with the added strength and weight and the added technique that has been taught by the coaches at each level, a player delivers and receives the results of those collisions routinely during games without giving it a second thought. It is particularly true in games, rather than practices, for two reasons. First, there is something on the line in each play which can lead to a change in the outcome of the game. A missed tackle, a sloppy block, or a forgotten assignment can mean a long run or an interception by an opponent or a fumble or a sack against your own team. Each play is a potential disaster for a team if any of these things happen. In the season, the players on the field are in a high state of awareness that they must at all times give their assignment and their execution their full attention and effort. The second reason is the presence of adrenaline in the systems of the players on the field, released by their bodies whom a state of combat regimens is in order to enhance the physical state they will need for a stressful and combative situation.

The four players trudging to the Phi Delta Theta home had been in these physical and emotional states for two and a half hours and were just now coming down from practice. They were physically and mentally exhausted. The good thing about it was that each man knew how the others felt, just like him. Silence was not only forgiven during the walk, it was expected and appreciated.

They went into the back door of the fraternity and headed to the kitchen. Cooksie, the fraternity cook, had made a large platter of ham and cheese sandwiches and had filled a large mixing bowl with fruit, all of which was found in the refrigerator. There was a handwritten message on a sheet of paper taped to the refrigerator door: *Food inside is for football players. Do not touch.* The Phi Delta Theta brothers had left the food alone over fear or respect, who knows why, but they had left it alone. Also in the refrigerator was a big pitcher of iced tea with lemon slices to wash down the sandwiches and fruit. The players each grabbed a plateful of food and a glass of iced tea and retreated to the dining room where they ate.

Alcott spoke first. "Cooksie, I love her. If she was younger and better-looking, I'd ask her to marry me."

Everybody laughed. Young shot back, "If she was younger and better-looking, she could do a lot better than you." More laughter.

The players started to relax a little and talked about the game and some of the plays, good and bad. They all knew which ones they were.

Finally, Ed Gardner got around to the subject of Ted Crouch. "Do you think Crouch intentionally hurt the wide receiver from Wesleyan?"

Young was the first to respond. "What do you think? Of course he did. He was burned so badly by the guy last year. He lost his start job, and nothing indicates he will get it back any time soon. I've played with him long enough to learn he can bear a grudge and have a mean streak. This was the perfect payback opportunity, and he took advantage of it. I hope this refocuses him. The Wesleyan player was not a bad guy, he is probably a good guy. The trouble is, he was the guy who showed up Ted's shortcomings, and Ted suffered the consequences, so he paid the price. Things like this happen every day in life, and they go unnoticed. This happened in front of a stadium full of people who all noticed. But it's over. Nothing can change it. Crouch will play more football this year in whatever role the coaches choose to put him in, because he plays hard and is a good man. Then he will graduate and get on with his life. I hear he is already interviewing with Proctor and Gamble in Cincinnati. The Wesleyan player? Same thing. He will heal. Even though he is done in college football, he will get a degree from a very good school and will get on with his life!"

As it turned out, Young was right. Matthews, the injured Wesleyan receiver, went on to become a sportscaster and broadcast the Kansas City Royals games on the radio for twenty-five years before he retired.

The four players gratefully finished the food Cooksie had so thoughtfully put aside for them and stacked their dishes in the oversized kitchen sink after they rinsed them off.

Suddenly, I got an idea. "Say," I started, "my roommate, Morgan, has a small refrigerator in our room with some beers in it. It was hot out there today, and you guys look thirsty. How about we have one each, just one? So long as I replenish them, he will be fine with it."

I instantly knew I had made a blunder when I looked at the faces of my three teammates. Blank, contained stares would be a good way to characterize their expressions. Not only did the coach have rules in effect about no alcohol, but Alcott was one of the team captains. All three players had a good chance of making all-conference this year, which was a big deal. In prior years, when I wasn't getting into any varsity games, some of my fellow benchwarmers and I would have a beer or two during the season; not many, but a few. It suddenly occurred to me that this was different from my past semester, a lot different.

My teammates' responses were firm but not judgmental. "No, thanks. It's nice to offer, but we are tired," Alcott said. And then, looking me in the eye, he continued, "Plus, there is a no-drinking rule, which not everybody follows but is expected to follow during the season, so I think we should follow it now, don't you?"

I was red-faced by the stupid question I had just asked my three varsity teammates. I just watched this awkward situation to its end.

"Yeah," I responded, "I got it. Stupid question to ask. Sorry."

Ed Gardner slapped me on the back. "Don't be sorry, Charlie. You were just being a good guy. You are a good teammate and will be a big contribution for us this year. It's just that things will be different for you, and at the end of the season, you will be glad they were."

"You are right, Ed. Thanks." I meant it.

They all went their separate ways, Alcott and Young to study, Gardner to drop by church, and me back to my room to rest my emerging aches and pains and to get a couple of hours of sleep. As my head hit the pillow in my air-conditioned room, I thought of my good future and the opportunity I had at this point in life.

CHAPTER 23

BUS TRIPS

In the Indiana Collegiate Conference, the farthest any two schools are apart is about three hours by bus, making trips between the schools for conference pretty much easy and convenient. If DePauw played an away game against a conference opponent that was scheduled to start with a night game before 6:00 p.m., the team would dress for the game in Greencastle, take a bus to the opponent's school, and return by bus the same day; unless the trip home would get them back late at night, in which event, the team would spend the night at a hotel and return the next morning.

The Tigers all seemed to enjoy playing night games away, sleeping in the next morning, taking a leisurely trip home, and getting ready for an evening on their own campus. The bus ride away from DePauw allowed the players to choose between studying, conversing, or sleeping as ways to spend their time on these trips. The players had all been identified by their teammates as studiers, talkers, and sleepers when it came to their selections of seatmates for game trips, and they made sure they had selected a comparable teammate for each trip, depending on their own interests.

Most players didn't much care who they had as a seatmate, as they all knew and liked each other, so long as their interests in how they would spend their travel time matched up.

I liked to keep to myself when I traveled, but I usually dozed off when I could easily position myself between a studier and a sleeper.

The 1963 game with Evansville was a Saturday-night game with kickoff at 8:00 p.m., so the Tigers boarded the bus at 4:00 (already dressed), enjoyed prepacked meals at 5:00, and sat back to enjoy the trip to Evansville without much conversation after the meal.

I was not known for my conversational skills and was not the kind of guy to jabber a lot, so I was fine with my choice of seatmates.

The meal the team would enjoy had been prepared by the staff at the student union building, who usually did a good job and kept the college kids happy most of the time, so there was little complaining from the footballers as they dug into their meals of sliced roast beef on grainy bread and a fruit cup with cookies. After the team finished eating, the talkative players engaged in subdued discussions, so as not to disturb the others, and the remainder quietly pondered their thoughts or fell asleep.

Meredith was one of the sleepers and soon fell into an unconscious state, leaving me to ponder things as the bus sped down the interstate toward Evansville. The temperature was in the mid-fifties, typical of the nighttime temperature in Central Indiana in late October. The planned route to Evansville did not go through many metropolitan areas but instead followed a course that went through farmlands and smaller towns to get to the Tigers' ultimate destination in plenty of time to empty the bus upon arrival and warm up for the upcoming football contest.

I did not fall asleep, like many of my teammates had done. Instead, I peered at the window into the cool night air and watched the buildings and the farmland go by as the bus proceeded on its way south. It was a crisp, cloudless night in Central Indiana, with the still country air thick with the occasional smell of burning leaves and cow manure, as the bus passed through the countryside, bathed in darkness, on its way to the team's destination.

As I lay my head back on the headrest, I thought about the things that were going on in my life and the things I expected to come. Here I was, a little more than halfway through college but still with no clue about what I would do after it was over. I had arrived at psychology as my major because I had been required to declare something at that point and held a fascination about the field of human behavior. But I didn't know that the mastery of that subject would provide me with the knowledge and skills I needed to maneuver through life. I knew that I had to do something to provide myself with a living for myself and for my family, since I intended to marry someday and to have children to raise with the woman I would marry.

All of this thinking was starting to distress me, and it caused pangs of anxiety and insecurity to well up within me as I thought about these things all the more while the bus headed on toward its destination. Eventually, I thought to myself that although the plans and events I had been thinking about were noble and important subjects, many of them were a long way off, and I had plenty of time to think about each and every one of them. Many of them might not occur at all, for one reason or another, so there was no point in thinking about them now. I had a football game to play tonight, with new plays to remember and information about the Purple Aces that might be contained in the reports of the coaches who had scouted them, and that was what I should concern myself with.

The game played that night by the Tigers was not very impressive, probably because of the length of the bus ride and the late starting time of the game. The team, which was out of sync, allowed Evansville, a middle-of-the-pack performer in the Indiana Collegiate Conference, to score fourteen points and only scored seven points itself. It was not great, but at least the team slept soundly on the way back to Greencastle.

CHAPTER 24

≡ 🏈 ≡

TWO-A-DAY PRACTICES

I WAS THE FIRST TO WAKE up, probably because my eyes were the first to be hit by the rising sun, due to my bed's placement in the dorm room where three of my teammates slept. It was 6:30 a.m., and as I rose out of bed, I could tell that the day would be just like the several that had preceded it. I could almost see the hot, stifling air rise out of the baked ground into the still atmosphere that would be there all day and all night. While the sun was in the process of coming up, I could see the clear sky overhead and realized that there was unlikely to be even scattered clouds in the sky, much less any semblance of a cloud cover that would provide any relief or protection from the blistering rays that had dogged us during the first week of the two-a-day practices and was bound to do so again in the second week.

My three teammates and I (who shared the dorm room for the two-week period) had watched a movie in the bum room of the Sigma Nu house where we were staying, and we had dragged ourselves up to our room at 9:30 p.m. By 10:00, we were all fast asleep, exhausted by what we had gone through that day, so as usual, we were too tired to shut the curtain to our dorm room. Not that it would have mattered, because as soon as one of us got up and started to move around the room, the rest woke up and started to get ready for the day. There was an advantage to being the first man up and the first to use the small bathroom adjoining the room.

As the school did every year, it assigned the football team one of the twelve or so fraternity houses on campus, which the school rented for us during the two-week period before the opening of school when the team had its two-a-day practices. The team members stayed two or three to a room in the same rooms that would be occupied by the members of Sigma Nu during the ballers of the year. When the Sigma Nus stayed there, it was two to a room, much more spacious than the two or three to a room for bigger occupants on the football team. I didn't know why the arrangement was what it was, but I surmised that this crowded setting was intended to make things less comfortable and maybe tighter for the football occupants of the packed rooms. The rooming strategy was to put all of the players who played the same position in the same room, presumably so they would talk about the plays with the blocking assigner for the position during their spare time. I was assigned a room with two other offensive halfbacks (like me), and the talk among the three players relating to plays and blocking assignments for the halfback division was sparse, far behind even the subjects of existentialism and the gross national product, which meant not at all.

Of the two (often halfbacks) I roomed with, who were seniors, both were ahead of me on the depth chart; and the sophomores were bigger than me and not as fast but were ahead of me in the depth chart.

By the time I was a junior, I had paid my dues as a sophomore, playing rarely in games except when the team was way ahead (which was not often) or way behind (which, fortunately for the team, but not for my playing time, did not occur much), so I pretty much limited my football sophomore year to practicing in the drills designed to enhance strength, stamina, and technique and by holding blocking dummies for practices of play execution by the first- and second-strings. I figured it was all part of a natural and gradual progression that all players go through. I knew it was not a certainty, however, because progress can show itself at any time. A younger player could always blossom and leap over the players in front of him and pass them up in a depth chart. Also, players on the depth chart could simply fail to mature or progress to the next level and remain stuck in place with little hope of progression. It could happen at any time, and it often did. It was rare that a player progressed beyond where he had been after the first month of his junior year. That's why the two weeks before classes started were so important to me. I knew I was lost enough and had proven myself enough to the coaches that I would have a reasonable chance to play on special teams, particularly as a kick returner and as a punt returner, but I was hoping for more. I wanted to get some playing time in as a full-time halfback, running the ball from scrimmage, catching passes, and of course, blocking for those who were running or catching or throwing passes. The only way I would do that was to show the coaches that I had improved in these areas over the summer since spring practice, when I had played third-string and second-string at times, but I thought I had put in enough weight and had gained enough speed to make an impression on the coaching staff. The only other way, and it was a bad way, was for one of the players ahead of me to get hurt and for me to take the place of the injured teammate. No player really wanted to advance on the depth chart the second way because it was preferable to progress as a result of an injury to a better player, which hurt the team and lessened its chances of success. Nonetheless, football is a violent game, and injuries are common, so every player had to be ready to step in for a fallen teammate at any time, and most were ready to do so (or at least thought they were). The two players expected to be the starting halfbacks were Bronson Davis (a big, fast transfer from Northern Illinois University) and Rene Bichet (a gritty, tough runner and blocker from McKees Rocks, Pennsylvania, who had played a lot as a junior). My objective was to be able to substitute for either of them during a game in case the need came up.

The daily routine called for breakfast between 7:15 and 8:10 a.m. at the student union building, followed by a chalk talk from the coaches in the team room from 8:00 to 8:45. The half an hour it took to walk to the practice field and get dressed and then practice from 9:15 to 11:30 (in 85°F weather) was followed by showers, then lunch at 12:15, some free time on campus or taking a nap at the Sigma Nu house, then another two and a half hours of practice from 2:00 to 4:30 p.m. When the morning practice ended at 11:30 a.m., the players simply took off their practice uniforms in the field and laid them out to bake and dry in the sun until the afternoon practice. They would be washed at the end of the week. On the other hand, jockstraps and socks were washed after every practice and replaced with new ones, so basic principles of hygiene were properly being adhered to.

All in all, it was grueling, uncomfortable, and draining, but it was necessary. There were two weeks of two-a-days, followed by one week of regular practice, and then by the first game where the Tigers would host Illinois Wesleyan, a school about the same size of DePauw that had beaten them by a couple of touchdowns in the previous season.

This particular morning, the players had dragged through breakfast, perking up only when somebody played Bobby Bare's "Detroit City" on the jukebox located in the students' dining area. The song blared out, "I wanna go home. I wanna go home. Lord, how I wanna go home." Most of the players nodded their heads and smiled in agreement. Some players even mouthed the words in support of the sentiment, which was clear. After more than a week of two-a-days in the oppressive heat with no one around but the other football players, they had hit a wall. Important or not for team-building and conditioning, they were tired and spent, and it showed.

All of this was not lost on the coaching staff. The same conditions always set in around this time at every set of summer two-a-days, and it was the coaches' jobs to pick up the pace and increase the interest level of the players. This would be accomplished by changing the drills the team went through after the calisthenics used for warm-up.

Coach Mont walked into the coaches' room to face the sixty-six players who had walked over from the student union building. Some were already noticeably sweating.

"Men!" he shouted. "Welcome to the second week of practice, your last week of two-a-days, if it means anything."

There was some polite laughter, but not much. Nobody wanted to demonstrate to the coach that the two-a-days were getting to them or that they weren't tough enough to handle them.

"I know these two-a-days are tough, but I want you to be tough, all of you. What you do in Norfolk gets you ready to do what you need to be able to do in October and November." Coach Mont noticed that the players all had made eye contact with him at the last sentence. He continued, "Believe me, this has been only a week, and all we have done is drills. Yes, you have been wearing pads and helmets, but that was only to give you the feel of wearing them. We have not used them for what they were designed for: contact. And contact will be a big part of how you prepare for the season and what you go through during the season. You will be playing the likes of Ball State and Indiana State this year." He was referring to two of the bigger schools and stronger teams in the conference. "They are bigger than you, and maybe faster and stronger than you. There is nothing you can do about that." The players' eyes were now riveted on him. "But they aren't tougher than you, unless you choose to let them be. That, men, is what you do have control over. You all know that contact is a part of this game, and you all know how to initiate and react to contact. You are football players. You have been trained for contact. Starting today, and until the kickoff for the first game, contact will be a part of everything you do, and the coaches will be watching and evaluating. Do I make myself clear?"

"Yes, coach," said Bill Alcott (the senior fullback/linebacker) and Ole Thomas (the senior guard), who were the captains of the team.

"Are Bill and Ole the only ones who know how to answer? Can anyone else answer?"

"Yes, coach," the team shouted in unison, their voices thundering.

"Well, then. On the field in half an hour," the coach shot back with a steely look. With that, he turned and walked out of the room, leaving the rest of them to sit in their chairs and glare at the chalkboard.

CHAPTER 25

LETTER JACKETS

At the conclusion of each season, the DePauw Athletic Department would put on an awards dinner for the football team at a local venue in Greencastle. At the dinner, Coach Mont recapped the recently concluded season and announced the most valuable player on the team (as determined by the votes of the players on the team), and there was a speech given by a sports personality, usually one from Indiana. In addition, the athletic director passed out the awards earned by the team members. These consisted of numerals given to the members of the freshman team, letter sweaters given to the sophomores who had played in at least half of the quarters of games played over the year, letter jackets earned by the juniors who had played in at least half of the quarters of games played over the year, and letter blankets to the seniors on the team.

Of all the awards passed out, the letter jackets were the most significant. They were made of heavy-gauge black wool with white leather sleeves and were emblazoned with a gold *D* in the front. In order to enable the recipients of the jackets to wear them comfortably over the winter, they were fully insulated, which meant they could be worn immediately on the day after the awards dinner and throughout the balance of the fall and winter, and that was exactly what happened. There were eight varsity teams at DePauw, with football being the largest, so the recipients of the jackets were a relatively large percentage of the student body and were easily spotted and recognized as they walked across campus each year.

Any athlete who earned a letter jacket at DePauw exuded the aura of confidence that invariably came with the jacket. It had a tendency to make him appear to be taller and stronger than before he began to wear it, and it showed. Once I received my jacket, I looked to see if I had caught the eyes of any coeds I had crossed paths with as I strolled the paths throughout the campus. I guarded the jacket with my life and took great pains to hang it as close to myself as I could wherever I went, as if it were my most prized possession, which it was, so long as I was in college. I was forever convinced that the jacket had dramatically improved my social life with the coeds from the manner in which I had received it.

CHAPTER 26

ALCOTT BACKS INTO A PROBLEM

THE GAME AGAINST BALL STATE was played in late October at Blackstock Stadium. The game was close, when it really shouldn't have been. Ball State had a team with large players on both offense and defense, and the game was not expected to be very close. A look at the crowd before the game led most of those in attendance to conclude that Ball State would win handily, despite the contest being a home game for DePauw.

Two of the better players for the Tigers were Brue Mackey, the quarterback, and Bill Alcott, who played fullback on offense and linebacker on defense, a legitimate two-way player. Both were on the punting team for DePauw, Mackey as the punter and Alcott as the blocking back. This duo had the difficult duty of getting punts off by Mackey without getting any blocked by Ball State's hard charging defensive linemen, and Alcott had to successfully block any Ball State lineman who broke through in an effort to block Mackey's punt. The tandem had performed well so far this year, with no punts having been blocked yet.

In the third quarter, after a failed third-down effort by DePauw, the Tigers lined up in punt formation. Mackey awaited the strap from ten yards back of center, and Alcott framed up five yards back of center to protect him from onrushing defense men. The snap came back clearly to Mackey on the two count, and Alcott took two steps back in order to hit any Ball State players charging Mackey, who proceeded with his punt, hit Alcott smack-dab in the rear end, and bounced off Alcott, hitting Mackey's punt back into his face, then rolled out of bounds. The whistle blew and the entire punting team of dejected Tiger players walked off the field in dismay and embarrassment. The DePauw crowd went silent as Ball State, cheering, ran out the clock and won the game from the Tigers.

CHAPTER 27

PLAYING IN
BLACKSTOCK STADIUM

I HAVE THOUGHT ABOUT THE FIRST game I've ever played in Blackstock Stadium. It was the home opener in my sophomore year against Centre College, a Presbyterian school of about 1,400 students, located in Danville, Kentucky, about 250 miles from Greencastle. It was a nonconference game, but the two schools had played each other off and on over the years, the last time being about four years ago. This was the first time I had played a game at Blackstock because the three games my freshman team had played the year before had been at Indiana State, Ball State, and Valparaiso (all away games), and I had been injured, having separated my clavicle in the first game of my freshman year at Indiana State. I became used to playing at Blackstock because the team practiced a lot there in the main stadium whenever the practice field became rock-hard because of extensive dry periods during the year. There were no sprinkler systems on the practice field like there were in the stadium, so the team just moved its operations to the stadium when conditions called for it, so as to avoid the dangers presented by scrimmaging on a surface with the resilience of concrete.

The game against Centre was a big deal for me and the other sophomores who were playing an official nonconference college game for the first time at Blackstock. We had all gone to varsity games our freshman year, but only as observers, since freshmen could not play varsity and could only play the freshman schedule of three games. As I walked into the stadium, I experienced the smell of freshly cut grass and the humidity of the freshly watered field. The chalk lines had been laid on the fields, and the goal lines and end zone markers had been set where they should be for the game. The vendor trucks were gathered around the south entrance to the building containing the home stands and were involved in the process of unloading the typical football fare that would be cooked in about an hour and sold to the hungry fans attending the game. It seemed automatic that everyone who attended a game at Blackstock, even if they had just finished a big meal before they came, had room for a steam-cooked hot dog, freshly popped popcorn, and a syrupy Coke served on ice in a large paper cup, which was the standard fare at Tiger games. The ticket booths, locked up all week, had their doors open and the operators could be seen inside, arranging their ticket spools and currency trays that soon would be operating in high gear.

Blackstock looked great, ready for another opener, ready for another season. It had been built in 1941 for $100,000 with a seating capacity of about 1,300. There were brick structures on the west side of the field where the supporters of the home team sat in the stands facing the field. The back part of the building contained the locker rooms for the home team and the equipment and uniforms for the players, as well as an area to store some of the maintenance equipment. At the tops of the stands was the protected press box and the area set aside for the broadcast of the games by the college radio station. The crowd could get to the restrooms, which were inside the building, by entering through the doors located at the south and north ends, which were opened at game time and stayed open for the duration of the game. Concessions, manned by student volunteers, were prepared and sold at a concession area inside the building. People had to stand in line for concessions, people stood in line to use the washrooms, and no one seemed to care. It was college football, and their team was playing well, so they were socializing. The outcome of the game was of secondary importance to them.

The visitors' stands across the field were built on a much smaller brick structure and probably had less than 1,000 of the 3,000 seats in Blackstock, with its own bathrooms. The visitors' locker facility was a separate brick building located in the south end zone and was rather small for a structure where thirty-five to eighty players would dress and shower before and after the games, but it appeared to function well. When my football career had ended, I realized I had never set foot in the visitors' locker facility, but I felt I had not missed anybody in the process. Each game in Blackstock was a separate experience I remembered, at least for a while.

DePauw's home games were pretty well attended, as a whole. DePauw was located in Greencastle, a town of about 10,000 in the middle part of the state, where farming was the way most people made their livings. There was a commercial area where the stores, banks, restaurants, and bars were located and were frequented by the occupants of the town but were vastly aided by the presence of 2,410 students, the faculty, and the support staff of the university. There were a number of factories and small-equipment suppliers in town, particularly related to farming equipment. At one time there had been a Coca-Cola bottling facility, which had closed down and lost some precious jobs, to the dismay of the community, but it was still getting by. The lack of better things to do on a Saturday improved the attendance at the football stadium, but seldom were all 3,000 seats occupied, except when DePauw played Wabash in their traditional rivalry game; and Butler, from nearly Indianapolis; and sometimes when they played Ball State or Indiana State. The student body was good about going to the games and cheering for the Tigers. It was a nice custom that a lot of sororities made sure their students showed school support by going to the games. This led to the natural consequence that a lot of male students came to the games to ogle or flirt with the sorority girls, all to the benefit of attendance.

While conference games usually resulted in the stadium being two-thirds to three-quarters full on average, the nonconference games, particularly against smaller school like Centre, did not generate much interest, and the Tigers were lucky to draw crowds to those games.

What did this all mean to the players? Any football fan flipping the TV channels on a Saturday afternoon would usually pick up a Big Ten game or a Southeastern Conference game played in stadiums with capacities ranging up to 100,000 in 1964. In these games, the level of energy was extremely high, even a couple of hours before kickoff, and remained that way throughout the game, both with the students and with the other spectators, a number of which were likely to be fueled by the countless types of alcoholic beverages available well before, during, and after the games. The palpating atmosphere of the games was noticeable throughout the contests. The crowd would cheer, boo, moan, or be involved in some type of expression with every play. The players who probably experienced the atmosphere of big-time football in their high school, as well as in college, were spurred on by the crowd's vocal reactions to each play throughout each contest. It was what they expected, what they had been promised, when they had signed on to play football. Frenetic fans were quite an experience, one which was frankly lived for by many throughout the week. For some fans, football didn't even matter if they were at a six- to eight-hour party, considering the buildup and the wind-down time for their own carnival atmosphere. For those who enjoyed the games, who actually followed and rooted for their teams, it was even better, a party and a meaningful enjoyment by the athletes from the schools they sponsored. The players were like rock stars and were treated the same way.

This was far from the world of small-college football players like those from DePauw and Centre, who would feel lucky to have 1,500 observers at their contest. There was a good chance that, for a number of players in each team, football would be a second activity for them long after time spent at the library or reading their course material for classes in the coming week.

The players who would take the field today for DePauw and Centre had a lot in common with those who would take the field in Lafayette, Indiana, later that day about two hours north of Greencastle for the game to be played between Purdue and Notre Dame. A number of them probably had been classmates, and surely a smaller number had even played against those who would play in the DePauw game. In high school, almost everyone went to the local public school in a town, so they all came from the same origination. The difference was the elite players were the ones who were invited to play in elite programs. The remaining players, if they wanted to play, were relegated to schools with football programs that were lesser renowned and probably smaller.

The bigger-name players were heavily recruited, had their education paid for, and were exposed to vast amounts of hype and publicity regarding who they were and their qualifications. They also had the experience of playing, if they were lucky enough to play in prestigious companies with well-known teams, and on TV to boot. The smaller-name players got none of this. Knowing that if he played, he would have to earn a scholarship if he couldn't get money from some source other than athletics, he would receive no accolades or publicity, and then he would be playing unknown teams at unknown venues at sparsely attended games was enough to dissuade many high school players from playing any further; so most did not continue to play. They had other things to do that would have a greater impact for what they would do with their lives, and they were right. There was no reward they could envision that would compel them to pursue the sport further, so many didn't, and they were right about choosing this course. The game had been good to them in high school, but they just didn't see the sense in taking in any further. The elite players didn't have a choice to make, really. Their education was paid for, they were on TV or were playing in front of 80,000 to 100,000 people on Saturday, and they were famous within their school or sometimes beyond that. Who would choose otherwise in this situation?

The ones that were not among the elite but who chose to continue to play anyway comprised the third group. They saw an intrinsic value in still playing the game in whatever environment they wound up in, each with his own reason. There was something in basic experience of playing the game and matching strength, conditioning, and cunning with the other team and with the man across from them that kept them at the sport, along with their teammates, trying to best a foe that wouldn't get on dominating them, that get free all the forces they could master in order to prevail in the contest. It did not matter whether there was 100 or 100,000 people there to observe the contest. All that mattered was generating and channeling the effort it took to win, and applying it so that they had their way. The fields may have been marked well or located within a comfortable stadium with all the amenities. All that mattered was that there was a place where the battle could be fought, and the opportunity was there to play the game to its conclusion. It was a chance to be a winner or a loser. Some managed to give up after a few games or a couple of years, realizing the futility of playing when nobody cared or would ever care. Others played every down they could in every game they could, just to continue the experience, to follow the process to its very end, because football players were what they were, first and foremost. Any game could be their last one. They were oblivious to what was or was not around them. They just played. They were not moved by the fact that their more glorious brethren played in packed stadiums with screaming fans, broadcast into homes by television, while they did not. They knew they would not do it forever, and that they could not do it forever, but they focused instead on the opportunity they had. It was football, and they had the opportunity to play, for which they were grateful.

It has been debated over the years whether playing a sport, particularly football, provides a player with better preparation in dealing with the challenges he will later face in life. To those who play it, the answer is yes. The adversities they face on the playing field are intent on having their way, dominating them, and ultimately beating them physically with whatever means they have. No nuances, no subtleties, no arguments; just brutal battle, most of the time legal. No player, no team, can ever let their guard down, relax, or daydream while on the field. Moreover, they have to rely on others and have to allow others to rely on them to prevail and to avoid defeat. Very few environments are like that for young men, with the attendant consequences either way. If you could master football, a bit of what life throws at you is manageable, and you don't need a cheery crowd to do this.

That's what playing in Blackstock was like for the young men who played in it.

CHAPTER 28

DON'T LET THEM KNOW WHEN YOU ARE HURT

WHEN I ASCENDED TO MY starting position with the varsity team, I was paired up with Bronson Doris, a senior who had played for two years at Northern Illinois University and had traveled to DePauw before his junior year. Bronson had a lot of speed and was a deceptive runner. He could also block pretty well. In his junior year, he had not played a lot because DePauw was two players deep on each halfback position, so he had to wait until he was a senior to get his chance.

He started out well and was a good runner in the Illinois Wesleyan game and in the Evansville game the following week, but he was hit in the elbow with a defense player's helmet in the Evansville game and experienced problems with the elbow which required some caution and protection from future hits. So, before the Ball State game the following week, he was fitted with a big padded device to be placed over the elbow area. Walt Sweeny, the trainer who constructed the device, had tried to keep it as small and unnoticeable as possible, but it just wasn't possible to do so.

Before the game started, Walt looked at Bronson and said, "I'm sorry, Bronson. I might just as well have painted a target on your elbow, but that's all I could do."

I had overheard this exchange and couldn't quite figure out what Walt had meant. It didn't take long into the game for me to comprehend what Walt had been talking about. It was like the pad on Bronson's elbow was a sugar cube in a swarm of flies, a place of destination for the Ball State defenders. Every time Bronson got the ball, the likeliest spot that was hit was his padded elbow. Sometimes it was the first thing hit, usually by the helmet of the tackler after a running start. Other times, when Bronson was tackled and was caught in a standing position by two or more players so that he did not go down right away, a defender would come into the scrum and hit the elbow with a helmet or a shoulder pad or would just yank the arm and jerk it hard while bringing Bronson down. The objective was clear: Bronson was an effective runner who added a lot to the DePauw attack, and if Ball State could hit him, all the better for them.

It worked. At halftime, Bronson, obviously in a painful state, sat in the locker room with his head down and with a big bag of ice around his elbow, with a glazed look on his face, staring in the general area of where Coach Mont was trying to give out the instructions to the team. His elbow had taken a terrific beating in the first half, and it showed. I wondered how long my teammate could take the pounding in the second half.

DePauw received the kickoff in the second half and proceeded to a ground game, moving the ball with pretty good success, and avoiding the passing game almost entirely. The ball was pretty much distributed to me, Bronson, and Bill Alcott, the fullback, in order to mix things up, with Mackey running the ball on a keeper once in a while after faking a handoff. Alcott got a lot of carries because he was a big, powerful runner with great stamina, and he was very effective that afternoon.

In football, nobody stands around. This is particularly true in the backfield where, if you are not running the ball, you are running interference and blocking for the runner at the point of attack; or failing that, you get a handoff or a pitchout, and you are running downfield to block a defender in that area. If a player just stands around, he is quickly corrected or pulled out of the game because he is going to get hit either way or is preventing things from happening.

Bronson was a good blocker, both at the point of attack and downfield where he could block well and sometimes spring a teammate who was running the ball an extra ten yards or so by taking out a defender. But today, on plays where it was his responsibility to block, he approached his job in slow motion, getting to his target late or sometimes not at all. He would wince when he made contact, and he could not hold his blocks very well, letting the defender slip by after the initial contact was made. It was clear to me (and to probably everyone else on the field) that the elbow injury and the abuse he had been receiving all afternoon had taken their toll and that with the application of a little more of it, something bad could happen.

It did. Bronson received a pitcher to take around the right side, and rather than lucky, the ball away with the right arm, keeping his body between the ball and the defender who would pursue him, he tucked it under the left arm, thinking that was the best way to protect it. A couple of snarling Ball State defenders caught up with him, and while the first wrapped him up, the second punched the ball out of Bronson's left arm, causing a fumble that the swarming Ball State team pounced upon. Bronson was back on the bench after the turnover and did not leave it for the rest of the game. Coach Mont had seen enough and put Rick Jordan, Bronson's backup, into the game in Bronson's spot on the next DePauw procession. Ball State would beat the Tigers that day by seven points. Bronson's plays and fumbles were not pivoted in the outcome, but they contributed, plus having an injured player on the field had its effect on the whole team. Without Bronson in there, we were not as good as we could have been, or so the players thought. This was not a good mindset in the game of football.

After the game, as I was walking back with Fox to our respective fraternities, both in a somber mood because of the loss, Fox said, "Do you think it was smart to bandage up Bronson's elbow before the game? Yes, it provided protection, but it let everyone know that he was hurt, and it fooled no one. Ball State just used him for target practice during the rest of the game. Without a pad on the elbow, no one would have known he was hurt, and he would have received less punishment if others didn't know about it. It was a bad decision to bandage him up that way. Maybe it was a bad decision to let him play." Fox was pretty beat up after a full afternoon of going head to head with the 260-pound Ball State defensive tackles and was in a state of exhaustion. All he could do was grunt. "Yeah, I guess so." End of conversation.

The experience had an impact on me. Sometimes you get hurt. *That's life*, I thought, *but if you let people know, more people will try to take advantage of it and will not try to help you. They figure they can exploit you and help themselves if they pound on your weakness or vulnerability until something happens. If you are tough and strong enough to fend them off, all the better, but it is probably a wiser situation never to let them know you are hurt in the first place, so they don't make the extra effort to make things worse for you or hurt you more.*

From that point on, I made it a point never to acknowledge an injury by putting tape on it or by limping or leaving the area where I had been injured. Whenever I carried the ball or was blocking, I would be the first to jump up after the play in a diminished or injured state; there was no reason to do that unless I had to. Human beings are competitive and opportunistic and can be expected to exploit weaknesses or vulnerabilities in one another if they think at all that they can benefit from them, so don't give any hints or signals that any weakness is there.

Maybe that was a jaded and distrusting way to look at life and other people, but I didn't think so. The memory of the Ball State players pummeling Bronson's injured elbow often came into my mind when the situation called for it as I was making decisions later in life that were complicated, as if to say to the other participants, "Is that all you've got? That didn't bother me or hurt me at all." I would do this no matter how painful the play had been for me, and many were painful. Did this have an effect on the opposing player? I didn't really know, but what I did know was that by withholding any indications that something the other guy did had achieved its intended effect, I deprived that player of the opportunity to consider that he had beaten me on a play. I also felt good about myself that I could put them off when I had to. It worked.

As I continued with school and with my career and proceeded through life, the principle of not letting others know I was hurt helped guide me and my actions. Sure, you have to tell your wife about things, and you should. Also, if someone is coming on you at full physical or emotional capacity and a lot is at stake in your performance, you need to tell them so they can explore their options.

CHAPTER 29

THE RED SHIRTS

On a beautiful spring day, I left the fraternity house for class. It was for psychology, and I was late.

At the end of my walk from the steps of the home to the public sidewalk, a handsome fellow with dark brown hair and a splendid shirt stepped up to greet me. "Hi," he said, flashing a broad-toothed smile. "You must be Charlie."

"Why, yes," I said in surprise. "Who are you?"

"I am Dan Crowfred from College Classics, the biggest college clothier in the area." He stuck his hand forward for me to shake, which I did. His right arm was festooned by a remarkable burgundy short-sleeve shirt. It was splendid, and I immediately stared at it.

"Do you like it?" Dan asked.

"I do, I really do," I answered.

"It is the bestseller of our spring line," he said, "a remarkable shirt."

"Yes, I can see that," I muttered, taking in the shirt. "Do you sell these shirts on college campuses?" I queried.

"Yes I do," Dan said. He looked back at me. "They are sixty dollars, but they are special. College guys love them. I was just at Butler and we sold out. Only a couple left, so I had to order some more from my company."

My eyes popped. "There were only a couple left? If I got one, I would be a star in demand on my campus," I said.

Dan assured me that would be, then he looked me in the eye and asked, "How would you like to be my special sales agent for College Classics for your house, Phi Delta Theta? You show the shirt to your brothers, you convince them to buy it, and you order it for them, then write a check to my company for sixty dollars and get a commission of ten dollars when the shirt comes in."

It worked out great. I wore the shirt that I wore around the Phi Delta Theta home for a couple of days, and I visited the brothers in their rooms. I just didn't tell the guys I sold the shirt to them. I was selling the red shirt to the other guys in the house, as well. This was probably a mistake.

On the day the red shirts that I had ordered for my brothers came in, I walked around the house and gave each brother the shirt he'd ordered. The delivery package came in at 10:00 a.m., and I made the rounds to deliver the shirts at noon.

At 1:00 p.m., the Phi Delta Theta brothers in the house all left to go to their afternoon classes. The problem was, more than half of them were wearing short-sleeve red shirts. This was a chaotic scene. They all concluded that, since they looked like members of the Russian soldiers of the Red Army, they had been duped, and they came looking for me in an angry mob.

I had to lay low for several days, and some brothers probably still have a grudge against me today, but they still looked great in their red shirts.

CHAPTER 30

THE PA ANNOUNCER CAUSES SOME EXCITEMENT

VALPARAISO UNIVERSITY CAME TO GREENCASTLE to play the Tigers on the first weekend in November. It's been said that, the Midwest can be beautiful in the fall when the sun is brighter, the air is crisp, and the trees are resplendent in the fall colors, but in November, their leaves just fade, the skies are constantly overcast, the temperature drops below any kind of comfort level (even with layers of clothing), and the precipitation takes the form of chilly, wind-driven rain. And this is usually the time when Midwesterners—who have spent their lives adjusting to changes in the weather and knowing there is nothing they can do about—start planning for several months of indoor living. Most of these folks do not mind, for it is part of the annual cycle to which they have become accustomed. The beautiful fields they have enjoyed over the summer and fall are required by Mother Nature to shut down in order to rest and recharge themselves over the winter months, and that's what they expectedly do. The residents who live in the area know that they must do the same thing during these months, if they are to tolerate their existence in this part of the country, and they do so without much complaining or remorse. Afternoons are devoted to the museums, libraries, movies, playhouses, coffee shops, restaurants, and bars that have played lesser roles in their lives in the warmer months; and for a good while, they welcome the change with enthusiasm, which admittedly never completely lasts all the way until spring.

On this particular Saturday, the rain had already been falling at sunrise—or at least at the time when sunrise would have occurred, if you could have seen it—and had been constant all the way until game time, even though it wasn't heavy. The temperature was in the mid-forties which, with the constant rain and the help of a westerly wind, made getting outdoors for a football game the least preferable of all the activities available to these people with the time or the opportunity to watch the Tigers play the Crusaders.

The equipment man broke out the rain parkas that had been in storage for at least a year, and he put them in the dressing room where each player could pick one up to wear during the game in order to protect himself. They were hooded coats, well-lined, with rubber extensions, and did an excellent job of shielding wearers from rain or cold. The players who were not in the game did not have to be told to hunker down on the bench, with their parkas buttoned and their hoods up, hands shoved deep into their parkas until they were called by Coach Mont to go into the game.

Usually, the players on the bench liked to turn back and peek at the crowd, trying to pick out some coed they knew and who might just have come to see them play. If there was no one special to look for, the players still liked to scope the girls in the crowd. They tended to dress up nicely when they went to the games since it was a good place to be seen and a good place to see the other girls and what they were wearing. Sometimes, they even watched the action in the field, but not often. The players didn't care who their mothers were; they were just glad the students were there, particularly the coeds, to cheer and root them on. Not today, however. The rain was steady, and the damp, cold air was oppressive, conditions that no college girl who had worked on her hair all week cared to face. The stands were virtually empty. I looked across the field and noted that the visitors' stands were also empty. Valparaiso University was only two and a half hours north of Greencastle, but that must have been where their students and parents were, even now, as their stands were even emptier.

The field was a quagmire at kickoff, and due to the constant rain that fell throughout the contest, things only got worse. The DePauw players were wearing black jerseys with gold lettering and white pants, and the Valparaiso players were wearing white shirts and white pants with black lettering; but by the end of the first quarter, all the players on both sides who had put in any meaningful playing time in the contest were caked with mud so as to make it impossible to see the colors of their uniforms, much less to see the numbers on their jerseys. The team members who were not in the game hunkered down in their waterproof parkas and hoods, and when the cold and water had saturated them, they improved their protection and comfort levels by grabbing any extra parkas that were stored and stacked on the benches, as well as any parkas that had been shed by the team members who were in the game. No one minded. The game was brutally conducted in the elements, with a ten-yard gain seeming like a fifty-yard achievement would have been in normal conditions. There had been very little scoring, with Valparaiso up seven-zero at halftime. It was impossible to determine who had started out with which parka, so the players going into the game just threw off the parkas they had been wearing and picked anything that was available off the ground when they came out.

It was different for the players who were not in the game, and a number of them took the opportunity to improve their personal situation and their comfort by picking up stray parkas that had been thrown off by game participants and putting them on top of the new one they were wearing. Several of the players who had been waiting on the bench had layered three or four parkas over themselves in an effort to stay dry and warm, giving them up only when one of their teammates coming off the field of play protested and demanded that they do so.

The game was close all afternoon, and halfway through the fourth quarter, it was still seven-zero Valparaiso. The rain had helped DePauw more than Valparaiso, since Valparaiso had a very good passing attack which was disrupted by the rain, making the game a lot closer than expected. Coach Mont was particularly energized by the closeness of the game, and he sensed the possibility of stealing a win that no one expected for the Tigers. He was nervously pacing up and down the DePauw sideline, planning ahead, hoping for a break, like a Valparaiso fumble, that would give the Tigers a chance at a touchdown and a chance at a two-point immersion for a win. Valparaiso had the ball on its own twenty-yard line, so the situation was ripe, if DePauw could get a break.

The public address announcers were a couple of students who had volunteered for the job. All they really did after each play was to say what the down was, how much yardage had been made on the play, who had gained the yardage on offense, and who had made the tackle or broke up the pass on defense. They had numerical rosters of both teams in front of them, so all they had to do was match the numbers of the players who had been involved in the play with the names on the rosters and announce the results. On this particular day, it was impossible for the announcers to be effective. The jerseys had been soaked, with several layers of mud on them, so they really couldn't call names with any degree of certainty or accuracy. By the fourth quarter, they were just guessing. On offense, where each team had one primary quarterback and three primary running backs, they had several names to pick from and usually guessed right. On defense, however, there were eleven mud-caked players trying to make the tackle, with no ability for the PA announcers to pick out who did what. Sometimes, the announcer would say a Valparaiso runner was stopped by "the DePauw line" or "the DePauw Defense," using a generic term, which was safe. Only when they clearly knew the individual who had made the defense play (which they sometimes did because they had followed the team all year) did they mention a specific name.

The next play was a second-down running play where the Valparaiso runner was hit and brought down by an alert Tiger tackler who had smelled out the play and executed his job peacefully. What happened after that was humiliating and embarrassing for those involved, but at the same time, it was hilarious in the way it played out.

Without hesitation, the PA announcer declared in the microphone, "That late tackle was made by Charlie Peck." The announcer was a member of the same fraternity as Charlie Peck, a seldom, if ever, used defensive lineman on the Tigers. No one ever found out whether the announcer just mistook the obliterated number on the tackler's jersey for that of Charlie Peck, or if he just wanted Charlie to hear his own name over the public speaker so that he would feel better. It didn't matter, because either way, Charlie was seated at the end of the bench, where he had been the whole game, safely tucked under a coat of three parkas to protect himself from the elements.

Nobody knew it, but Charlie had heard his name called, and it probably didn't matter. What did matter was that Coach Mont heard the announcement and immediately erupted in a loud voice, with an inflection partially of incredulity and partially of panic, "Charlie Peck! Charlie Peck? Oh my god, Charlie Peck!"

There were very few people in the stadium at that particular moment. Even though the game was still close, the rain, the cold, and now the wind (which had picked up) had driven out almost everyone in the stadium, except for the players, who had to be there. The result was that everyone who was still in the stadium heard Coach Mont's spontaneous outburst. Charlie Peck heard it and immediately thrust off his parkas, buckled the chinstrap of his helmet, and ran as fast as he could to the area where the coach was standing, waving his arms, trying to figure out his next move in light of the revelation that had just come from the PA announcer. Charlie was charged with adrenaline. He was a junior from Gary, Indiana, weighing 210 pounds, which was light for a defensive lineman, and had only made brief appearances in three previous games in the two years he had been on the varsity team. He never missed a practice, and he gave it his all on the practice field. Unfortunately, he was slow and not too talented, and he had never been chosen for the traveling team for the away games, but he suited up for every home game because there was no NCAA rule on how many players on the home team could dress for games. For his whole career, he was ready to jump into action when needed, and now, he thought, his time had come.

He ran up to the coach and exclaimed, "Here I am, coach. What do you want me to do?"

The coach looked back at him. Both surprise and relief were written in equal amounts on his face. What he said next could have been said differently—and doubtlessly would have, had the situation not been so stressful and surprising. "Oh, Charlie, thank God. When I heard that announcement, I was afraid you were in the game," the coach blurted out the words.

Everybody on the bench cringed and felt for Charlie at that moment. Most people diverted their eyes away from the coach and the player in order to avoid the discomfort.

Charlie just said, "OK, coach," and headed back to the spot he had occupied on the bench. Fortunately for him, the exchange happened so quickly that the three parkas Charlie had shed were still on the ground where he had thrown them, so he was able to reclaim them and stay as warm and dry as possible for the balance of the afternoon.

DePauw did not get its break for the rest of the game and did not score, losing seven-six. On Monday, the team showed up for practice, including Charlie Peck. He showed no residual effect from what had happened at the game, and he practiced as hard as anyone on the field, undaunted. Just like he had for the past three years.

CHAPTER 31

DISASTER AT BUTLER

ONE OF THE BIG GAMES for the Tigers each year was the one at Butler, a state school in Indianapolis with an enrollment of about 4,500 students. The campus was a short distance from DePauw, with a large enrollment of live-in students and those who commuted from the city from the areas surrounding the campus. It had a good academic reputation and excellent athletic teams for a school of its size. It had an enviable win/loss record with the Indiana Collegiate Conference and was particularly tough on DePauw in football and basketball over the years, starting in 1884, and its football team had won thirty consecutive games against the Tigers by the time the teams played in 1964 (my junior year) when Butler held a three-zero conference record by the time it took the field for the 1964 game against the visitors from Greencastle.

Butler played all of its home games in the Butler Bowl, an imposing facility on its campus where 50 percent of its playing field had been excavated to a level well below the ground level of the playing surface, an imposing drop off Butler's football games were will attended because there was a large population within the area surrounding the school. Basketball was the main sport at the school, which had regular contests with Indiana University, Purdue University, and Notre Dame, winning many.

The Tigers' trip to the Butler Bowl consisted of a forty-five-minute bus ride so, as with several other opponents in close proximity to DePauw (such as Wabash and Indiana State), the DePauw team dressed for the game at

Blackstock Stadium, rode the bus to the Butler Bowl, and returned after the game to Blackstock to take its program showers.

Coach Mont's pep talk prior to the kickoff contained the proper inspiration but was not boastful. The gist of it was that, while Butler had a strong team this year and was riding a strong winning streak against DePauw, they were beatable; and if the Tigers played as well as they were capable of, anything could happen. Coach Mont pointed out that the impressive size of DePauw's offensive line of Fox, Moore, Gardner, Johnstone, and Larson gave the DePauw running game an edge and could help the Tigers' running game today, for which he would rely on the tireless Alcott at fullback, me, and Bronson Davis (a transfer from Northern Illinois University) at the halfback positions, and Bruce Mackey (the nimble friend and shifty runner) at the quarterback position.

Butler, which won the opening toss, received the kickoff and returned it to DePauw's thirty-yard line before punting to DePauw on the fourth down. Bronson Davis took the punt and returned it fifteen yards, putting DePauw on its thirty-five-yard line, and then started to show its running game by having its big interior linemen block for its off-tackle plays, run up the middle, and sweep; then utilizing its running backs to move the ball down to the Butler five-yard line before Alcott ran the ball, untouched, into the Butler end zone. Although the extra point kick failed, DePauw enjoyed a six-zero lead, putting DePauw ahead for the first time in the series in who knows how many years, and the Tiger bench and coaching staff were ecstatic, sensing that they could accomplish something for the first time in the series in at least twenty-five or thirty years. Late in the second quarter, Butler—still behind at six-zero—had the ball and stalled on the fifty-yard line and sent in its punting team. DePauw sent Davis and me to serve as the deep backs to field Butler's punt, with both players above twenty yards apart on the DePauw fifteen-yard line.

The return play called for Davis to call out who would return the ball when it was in the air after the punt. Whoever was not returning the ball would block the first player from the kicking team who got downfield, and the return man would run to the gap created by the block to make the return.

CHAPTER 32

YOUNG AND ALCOTT TAKE THE MEDICAL BOARDS

WHILE PLAYING FOOTBALL WAS A special experience for the men who participated in that sport at DePauw, they were mostly at the school for the same reason: to obtain a degree in a field of study that enabled them to qualify for entry into a graduate school or a professional school that offered them the opportunity to obtain a degree that was beyond a college bachelor's degree. It was not lost on the football players that they were in college to go on to careers as academics, financiers, and doctors. And Phi Delta Theta's Stu Young and Bill Alcott, two of the starting linebackers for the Tigers, were examples of this type of student. Both were in the premed program and had already applied for entrance to medical school upon graduation. Young would go on to Indiana University to become a heart surgeon, and Alcott to Ohio State to become an orthopedic surgeon.

While they were successfully participating as members of the Tigers football team, they were putting in the hours of study and lab work required to graduate with honors, so as to achieve entrance to the medical schools of their choice and become medical doctors. Coach Mont and the teammates were not remiss in recognizing the grueling schedules each of them kept in order to make this happen. It didn't take much time for a

118

person to look into their faces and realize the seriousness with which they approached their athletic performances and their planned life's work after football was over for them. I, in particular, was aware of the way Young and Alcott were conducting their lives because both players were fraternity brothers of mine at Phi Delta Theta, and I had the opportunity to see the hours they committed early in the morning, before classes began, during the day, between classes, after football practice, and during the night to study hard and intensely from their textbooks and lecture notes about the human body. I figured that both players released the tension and the imbalances in their lives during the two hours per day that they were at football practice, when they used intense effort to block, tackle, and hit with all the authority they could muster. Sometimes I thought about it and just couldn't figure out how and why they approached their lives the way they did, day after day. It's not like I was a party boy. I was a serious student, like just about every player on the team. Most students at DePauw planned on continuing their education after achieving their bachelor's degrees in academics or one of the professions. I intended to follow the same path, once I figured out what I would do after graduation. I just needed to figure out what that path was. In the meantime, I just observed Young and Alcott, the doctors-to-be, and the observation was made with maximum amazement.

In the meantime, while I valued that premed players strived to exceed both in the classroom and on the football field, Coach Mont looked at the calendar from time to time and reminded himself continuously that, on October 10, his two prized linebackers might be missing from the team when DePauw played Washington University in St. Louis at Blackstock Stadium. On the day, when the rest of the team would be playing at 2:00 p.m., Young and Alcott would be taking the four-hour medical school entrance exam in Indianapolis that started at 9:00 a.m. and finished at 1:00 p.m.. This left the two players with one hour after the exam had ended to change into their football equipment and uniforms and drive to Blackstock in time for a 2:00 p.m. kickoff. To accomplish this, they had arranged for Young's father (who was a doctor) to pick up the two linebackers outside the testing location, and speed (without getting arrested) to Blackstock, where the players would jump out of the car, fully dressed, and be there for kickoff. It could be done, provided there were no surprises or delays of any type in the execution of the plan. If there were any delays, there would be plenty of trouble, since DePauw had no linebacking depth behind Young and Alcott, and Washington University had two very good receivers and an excellent running back. The consequences would be disastrous for the Tigers.

But Coach Mont had a plan. The way things work before a football game, whether high school or college, the two participating teams come out onto the field approximately forty minutes before the set time for kickoff, and each one takes an end zone where it does warm-up drills such as jumping jacks, leg lifts, neck drills, and running in place. They take about sixteen minutes to tend to this. Then both teams run some formation drills where they run plays for about ten minutes. Then each team retreats to their locker room, where the coaches go over the scouting report on the other team and the assignments they have come up with for their players for the game, followed by a pep talk by the coach and a short team prayer by the chaplain. The referee calls both teams to the field for kickoff and the two teams line up for kickoff, which takes place right after they line up. When Washington University came out, it completed the pre-kickoff routine, but DePauw did not. They didn't run onto the field for warm-ups until Washington had been there for fifteen minutes. Moreover, when the referee did not call DePauw onto the field, Coach Mont told them to sit quietly and say nothing, which they did, despite the initial call for them to take the field, and just sat there silently for twenty minutes after the first call to do so. The referee had made first, second, and third calls to take the field before Coach Mont told us to take it. By the time the third call was made, the tone of the referee's voice was extremely angry, with the kickoff coming a full ten minutes after the two teams ran out to the field and met within the time planned. Through the coach's delay tactics, the opening kickoff was at 2:45 p.m., and it was Washington University that was required to kick off. DePauw had managed to make the kickoff at 2:45 p.m. through its machinations and skullduggery.

DePauw's efforts to delay the kickoff by forty-five minutes allowed Young and Alcott time to get out of the car, scale the cyclone fence surrounding the field, and take their positions to run onto the field on the first play after kickoff. When the students' section saw the two players buckle their chinstraps and run onto the field when they did, a load of roars went up from the students' cheering section. It was only then that the

Washington coach realized how badly he had been duped. He immediately called time-out before the ball was kicked and ran onto the field to plead his case that DePauw had done something illegal and should be punished.

The referees—confused, and realizing the kickoff wouldn't take place until they'd adjudicated Washington's complaint, which could delay the cocktail parties and social events they had to attend that night after the game—ruled that nothing DePauw had done had been illegal. The Washington coach went into a rage, throwing his clipboard and hat on the ground and kicking both of them ten feet into the air, then releasing some sharp epithets at Coach Mont who just stood there with an amazed look on his face. The kickoff took place, and I took the kick and ran it to the twenty-five-yard line while protecting the ball and my private parts from the wrath of the Washington players, giving a sigh of relief. The only punishment received by DePauw was a rip in the football pants incurred by Alcott as he climbed over the fence. Even though Young and Alcott both played well, DePauw lost the game twenty-one to fourteen, and the Washington coach got his revenge, sort of by cancelling the next game with DePauw, which was to be played in St. Louis the following year. As it turned out, the cancelled game with Washington was replaced by a game to be played by DePauw with the Camp Lejeune Marines football team.

Butler's punt was high and long and over the heads of me and Davis. When Davis saw it was headed toward me, he shouted, "Charlie, take it!" So I backed up to take the punt. What happened next was a disaster.

The coaches had always told the punt returners not to field a ball that was coming down inside the sixteen-yard line. The reason was simple. A punt inside the sixteen was likely to roll into the end zone, resulting in a touchback with the result that the receiving team was awarded possession of the ball at its twenty-yard line with a first down and eleven yards to go. DePauw would have to put the ball in play by kicking off or punting to Butler from its own twenty, giving them the ball.

I was mortified. As I walked off the field before DePauw kicked, some of the players patted me on the back and said kind words like, "Shake it off," or, "Don't worry, we still have time," or "It can happen to anybody," or they just spoke words to me that were not kind. I quickly took my place on the bench and remembered to keep my head up rather than displaying total dejection, although I felt dejected. Fortunately, Butler did nothing with

DePauw's punt, and the team went off the field at halftime with DePauw still ahead six to two, but not feeling very good about it.

DePauw kicked off the second half, and Butler drove down the field with running plays, scoring the touchdown to make the score eight to six. They brought their extra point team onto the field to make the point after touchdown. I was secretly hoping for Butler to make the extra point, because if they did, my faults would not have determined the outcome; on the other hand, if the player receiving the punt dropped or fumbled the ball, the kicking team would likely recover the fumble and either score a touchdown or have possession of the ball inside the ten-yard line. Either one would be a bad result for the receiving team. If I had done what I had been trained to do, the ball would have gone into the end zone, and DePauw would have been awarded possession of the ball on its twenty-yard line, but regrettably, I didn't do what I was supposed to. I tried to catch the ball, but it bounced off my hands and into the end zone. A loud noise came up from the crowd, signifying that something significant had happened for Butler.

I looked over my shoulder at the ball laying in the end zone, and I intuitively ran back to pick it up to avoid a Butler touchdown. I accomplished this, but when I tried to run it out of the end zone to avoid a safety, I was hit at once by the Butler players, and I went down with both players trying to claw the ball out of my hands. The referee blew the whistle and raised his hands with his palms waving, signifying a safety and two points for Butler. Moreover (assuming there would be no more scoring), DePauw would have six points, and Butler would have nine points; a win for Butler by three points, no matter how you put it. If Butler's extra point had failed, they would have eight points to six for DePauw, a difference of two points, which would have been the two points resulting from my fumble, a horrible statistic because my fumble would have been the cause of Butler's win. I secretly thought, *Come on, make it,* when the Butler kicker's foot struck the ball and it sailed flawlessly through the uprights, removing a big burden from my shoulders, which would have lasted a lifetime. I gratefully exhaled, the blunder was forgotten by the team (mostly), and the Tigers began preparations for next week's game. *Events always have consequences*, I thought to myself as the bus headed for Blackstock. The final score was a bad event, but not a catastrophic one for me.

CHAPTER 33

HELMETS TELL THE STORY OF A SEASON

THE DAYS BEFORE THE WABASH game, after the last practice by the Tigers occurred, I took off my practice uniform, including my gear and my helmet, but gave things a thoughtful glance before stepping into the shower room. At that moment, I realized the story of the nearly completed season that the helmet told me. My helmet recounted the season in vivid detail with each smear of paint from the helmet of at least one of the players from each of the opposing teams DePauw had played that season. Some were prominent and had resulted from a significant collision between my helmet and the helmet of an opposing player, like the blue streak caused by the linebacker from St. Joseph's who had knocked me unconscious, and the red streak caused by the blocks I had made on the defensive end of Ball State. There were others, particularly from Indiana State and Valparaiso. Other smears were not as pronounced, and just looking at them and remembering some of the plays that had caused them brought back memories of the games they'd resulted from, sometimes vividly, like how I felt about each of the plays.

The smears would be removed from the helmets in the offseason by the paint and polish remover applied by the employees of the DePauw Athletic Department who conditioned the helmets for use the following year. The new players who received the reconditioned helmets had no idea who had used them the previous year and what plays the helmets had been involved in. Those plays were kept alive only in the memories, aches, and pains of the players who wore the helmets, but they would exist for a lifetime. Looking at this year's smears, I realized a similar story would be told by his helmet, reconditioned this year and made ready for the new hits that would be made next year and would result in new stains, replacing those that had been sustained by time and would now disappear forever, along with the stories behind them. Almost every mark had a story behind it. The painful lights one roll resulting from the hit by the middle linebacker from St. Joseph's, the twisted knee resulting from the shot to my right leg by the diving tackle made by the Illinois Wesleyan defense, each one bringing back a vivid memory from a particular play, not to be forgotten.

As the marks on the DePauw helmets demonstrated, the marks that come with each play comes more prominently with the passage of time as each play was executed were more pronounced for each play. The significant ones lingered as I thought more about them. Some would be soon forgotten from that point on, and some would stick for a while.

CHAPTER 34

PRESENTATION OF THE PSYCHOLOGY PROJECT REPORT

Fox AND I BOTH TURNED out to be psychology majors. While we were good friends and teammates, we did not go through college joined at the hip. Each had his own interests and his own set of friends, and it was a good way to be. We socialized together quite a bit and enjoyed each other's company, but in proper doses. Each chose his own separate fraternity house to pledge and went about his business with the brothers in his own house. It wasn't a surprise, however, that each of us separately decided on psychology as a major, as we were both fascinated with human behavior and behavioral science and had talked about the subject in high school and in early college years. Fox and I did not find ourselves in the same psychology courses until junior year when we both signed up for a class in the psychology of advertising. We both looked forward to it because it was taught by Professor Kelly, who was very in tune with the students and had a large following. The class was famous for putting its students in groups of three, allowing each group to select a product to create an advertising campaign for and then present the campaign to the entire class as a group. Friends who had taken the class before told us how much fun they'd had, so Fox and I were really looking forward to it. We decided at the outset to be in the same group. For our third member, we invited Anthony Long, one of Fox's fraternity brothers in the Beta house who was also in the class and had been Fox's roommate in freshman year. I liked Anthony and thought he was a good guy, so the group was quickly assembled.

One thing I had not considered was that in making my selection of a team, I would be putting a great deal of pressure on myself. While Fox and Anthony were good friends of mine and great guys, they were not particularly devoted students, and each of them spent as much time playing cards, watching TV, and drinking beers as they did studying. It was not a good recipe for academic success and was proven by the fact that both of them had grade point averages of about 1.9 out of 4.0, which meant that each had to get at least some B's and no D's for their final two years, in addition to the C's they expected to make, in order to graduate with the minimum 2.0 average necessary to obtain a degree rather than just a certificate of attendance. A's were realistically out of the question. I knew that only so much effort could be expected from Anthony and Fox in the project, so if it was to come from anyone, it had to come from me. I was OK with it, though. I would do it for Anthony and Fox, but the pressure was on me.

The product chosen by our team for the project was a polishing product for brass called Bar Keepers Friend. We'd found it in a trade magazine and took an immediate liking to it because of the name, which was resonant with some of our interests. Advertising for the product was conducted in small newspapers and brochures, which was not much, and we were left with a wide open field to put our imaginations to work. The assignment consisted of laying out an advertising campaign, selecting target recipients of the ads, selecting the media in which the ads would be presented, creating copy and graphics for a typical advertisement for preparation, and coming up with a budget. *Just like the big guys on Madison* Avenue, I thought.

The term was ten weeks long, so we had plenty of time. Our project would account for 50 percent of our final grades, in addition to the 50 percent attributed to our midterm and final exam grades, so there was plenty of pressure for the project to be good. We got organized early in the process. Fox designed a target list to the campaign, selecting the media in which it would be presented. Anthony, who had taken some art classes, designed a new can for the product and the leisure character, which was a heavyset bartender with a plaid vest, suspenders, a handlebar mustache, and a wide grin. And I slapped together badges made largely from my own thinking and from a rate sheet for ads that I'd obtained from one of the newspapers in Indianapolis. It was an amateurish effort, but an effort nonetheless. All that was left was to create a slogan and a theme. This would make the difference in our quest for a B, which was so desperately sought by Anthony and Fox. We continued to meet on Monday nights for the full term. Sometimes we would talk about the project, sometimes about football (which Fox and I played; Anthony did not, but was knowledgeable and had his opinions about football generally and the Tigers in particular), and sometimes about life in general. Anthony had a small refrigerator in his dorm room where he kept beers, so once in a while (not often), we would each have one to end the meeting. One night, Anthony ended the meeting by announcing it was the last call. Suddenly, I exclaimed, "I've got it. Bar Keepers Friend: good beyond the last call." Buoyed by the beer we had just consumed, and by a desire to get the project completed, we rejoiced. We had closed the loop. We had the theme and the slogan. We were in the home stretch.

There were eight groups in the class. Two groups would present each week, since class was about one hour long. Dr. Kelly had told us how it would work. A team would present all aspects of its project, then Dr. Kelly would ask questions. He was a nice guy, and everyone knew that with any level of common sense, a team could answer his questions, which were not complicated, tricky, or mean-spirited.

Our team was ready to go in the first week and wanted to be called. As fate would have it, when he asked who would like to go, he was looking at the left side of the room where Julie Winston, Elizabeth Williams, and Sara Fuller—all members of the Kappa Kappa Gamma sorority—shot up their hands. Fox, Anthony, and I were on the right side of the room, but we were the only two groups that wanted to go first. "Alright," exclaimed Dr. Kelly. "Ladies first. Gentlemen second."

At first, I was miffed. "Damn Kappas," I muttered to myself, "They won't accept when I ask them over on dates, and now they do this to me." I was right with my facts, but that was no concern between the two groups. Then I got to thinking, *Maybe it is better to see one of these and to know what to expect than to be blindsided along something we were not prepared for*, so I just sat back to watch.

Kappa Kappa Gamma girls in most schools are bright, good-looking, well-kept, and well-dressed and could be seen by some as hard to approach. This was why I'd rationalized my lack of success in dating them. The product chosen by the three girls was a new kind of shirt designed in New York, which was worn by all the high-fashion types, young and old. *Not much imagination*, I thought, *but probably safe.* Their presentation was OK but not particularly inspiring. The copy and the graphics they laid out for magazines like *Vogue* and *Mademoiselle* were predictable and vanilla, but designer clothes were the world in which the girls lived, and they were very enthusiastic in their discussion of the product. When they finished, Dr. Kelly asked a few well-intended, nonthreatening questions that were quickly answered. Everybody figured their part was over, and we got ready to take a five-minute bathroom break before the Bar Keepers Friend presentation.

Suddenly, a voice came from the back of the room. "Excuse me, but we have some questions we'd like to ask. Since this is something of a competition, we think it's only fair for the rest of the class to make some inquires of them."

Everyone looked up. The voice that had spoken was that of a member of the Roberts Residence Hall, which was notorious for winning (or nearly winning) the collegiate academic award every year, and for producing annually a group where thickset, horn-rimmed glasses were a standard part of the daily dress. Seated next to him were two fellow Roberts members who were part of their team.

"Well, this is a bit unusual, and it has not happened before, but it's all part of the learning process, so why not? You girls don't mind, do you?" the Roberts speaker asked.

If I had looked carefully into the eyes of the Kappa girls, I would have immediately spotted their looks of terror and panic and might have reacted differently to the question. Julie and Elizabeth couldn't speak. Sara could barely squeak over out an OK.

"So go ahead, ask some questions, but no more than five minutes' worth," Dr. Kelly allowed.

The look on face of the Roberts speaker (and to a slightly lesser extent, the faces of the two cohorts) resembled the expression of a jackal approaching a small pork chop. The attack was sudden and devastating in every respect.

"Why did you choose such an easy subject?" "Was there any research about what the target group would be, or were you just continuing with the will to please rich girls?" "Aren't there any media outlets besides *Vogue* or *Mademoiselle* that you can think of?" "You have left us without any conclusion projection or statistical analysis in support of your conclusions. Is there any reason for this?" The Roberts guys shouted out each question without even waiting for an answer. They didn't have to; they knew there would be none. The Kappa girls were trembling, unable to utter a word if they wanted to, but there was nothing to say.

"Whoa, just a minute. I think this has gone a little too far." Dr. Kelly's voice broke the onslaught, just like he had jerked on the leash of a pit bull. He continued, "The grade a group gets is its grade, the grade it deserves. If possible, everyone could get an A, or everyone could get an F. There is no bell-shaped curve here, so there is no advantage to be had in tearing down another team's presentation. I know what to look for, and whether I've found it."

The Roberts guys looked back at him with smirks on their faces. They had done what they thought had to be done with the Kappa girls, and they were fully prepared to do it again to others if they thought it was to their advantage.

Dr. Kelly called for a five-minute break before the next presentation. As he got up to leave, I took note of the Kappa girls, who were sitting motionless at the lectern table. No one was speaking, but both Julie and Elizabeth were dabbing their eyes with Kleenex and were fighting back little sobs.

Fox had a funny look on his face as he went out to the hallway. He didn't appear to care whether Anthony or I was with him. He was heading for the Roberts guys, who were standing around taking a cigarette break and saying a few things to each other, then laughing. I hurried out to where Fox was approaching, and I thought I had better be there, just because Anthony was right behind me. The Roberts speaker was the first to see Fox. He motioned to the other two, and they all were quiet by the time Fox got there.

"Nice questions, guys. You really took care of those Kappas," Fox offered.

"Yeah, they really hadn't put much effort into their work, and it was obvious. We had to show them up," said the speaker. The other two looked worried. If the speaker couldn't guess what could happen next, they had, and they looked plenty worried.

"Well," said Fox "we are next, and there will be no questions. Do you get me?" As he said it, he pounded his right fist over his open left hand four or five times. The sound of a fist hitting flesh was impossible to miss or take lightly. Fox had been an all-conference offensive tackle last year and would repeat it this year. He was six feet three inches tall and weighed 245 pounds, which was huge in 1964, even if it isn't now. The guys in the Roberts group were smart, and the message they'd just received would have been clear to anyone. Fox's message had been delivered with such conviction that there was no doubt as to whether he meant it or what he would do if questions were asked after the presentation. Everyone slowly returned to the classroom.

Dr. Kelly introduced me, Fox, and Anthony and took the opportunity to admonish the class. "We have allowed students to ask questions of the presenters and will continue to do so in order to be fair to everyone, but I must ask that the question remain civil. Is that clear?"

Everyone nodded, including the Roberts group. Kelly looked relieved, but he was still apprehensive.

The presentation went fine. Every one of the group members who spoke, especially Fox, looked composed and comfortable. We did a pretty good job.

Dr. Kelly didn't even ask questions. He just said, "Are there any question for the class?" Nobody said anything in response. He repeated himself, this time directly to the Roberts group. "Any questions? Last chance." The Roberts group sat stiff and frozen, looking straight ahead with their arms pinned to their sides. "Very well, then. Class dismissed. Two more reports next week."

Fox, Anthony, and I picked up our report and exhibits and headed for the door. We would get our B on the report and for the class, and Fox and Anthony would get their degrees—barely. Fox had overcome a big obstacle that day, and I was all the more thankful for the way Fox could open up holes for me on the left side of the line the same way he could handle other obstacles in the classroom.

CHAPTER 35

COACH MONT RUNS FOR CONGRESS

It was the winter of 1964, and most folks in Greencastle were stuck in the normal rut hat beset them at this time of year. Except for the hardiest of them, people had directed their activities to the inside varieties, and their time out of doors was limited to scrambling to and from their cars, which would take them to places where they wanted to be or where they had to go, places of employment being the most prominent. Occasionally, there was an outdoor activity, such as getting a car out of a snowbank; but usually, those were quickly performed so that those involved could go back to the warmth and routines they sought for themselves during the winter months. College students were the exception to the rule, because for the most part, they did not have cars, and walking was their sole means of transportation on campus. It wasn't so bad at DePauw because the campus was within about an eight-block radius containing the academic buildings, the library, the living quarters, and the living units. The sole exceptions were the fraternities, such as the DKE's, that chose to be a little farther off campus, for some unexplained reason. Maybe they liked the extra exercise they got when they walked to campus four blocks father than others did. Maybe they thought that being so far away from campus made it less likely that they would be subjected to the surprise visits from school security that would occur from time to time on living units (the

131

most frequent occurrence at the fraternity houses which had calculated a likely for beer and made the consumption a big part of their college experience). *Who knows*, I thought, *the DKE's are all a little crazy anyway.* (Which they were.) The rest of the student body usually stayed within the normal radius of the campus. They walked to and from their activities all the time, but they walked a lot quicker in the hard winter months. The cold was brutal, and the coeds were bundled to the hilt in parkas, leaving nothing more interesting for the male students to ogle at than they would at a walrus or a bear.

While you could not exactly call Indiana a politically active state, the time spent in the late winter months sometimes shifted to politics, due to the desperation which came from the lack of better things to do, and due to the fact that the party primaries which produced the candidates for state, local, and federal office that would run in the following fall took place at this time. The primary sometimes produced some surprising candidates, files were appeared normal day the rest of the year, but emerged as a candidate when the primary took place for one or more reasons, ranging from a newly acquired desire to serve, a new conversion with a political group, or in most cases, sheer boredom. It didn't cost anything to get on a ballot, just the registered number of signatures and a filing fee, so a number of people took the plunge, even in Greencastle.

Everyone was shocked in the early winter of 1964 when Coach Tommy Mont announced he intended to run in the Republican ticket for Congress, seeking the seat that would be given up by Representative Frank Zeller, who had held it for ten years but was retiring and had put in enough years to qualify for a good pension.

Anyone who knew Coach Mont might have been a little surprised by his announcement, but those who knew him well (like his players) were not shocked. The coach was not atypical of those men in his profession. He was stoic, structured, and disciplined; possessed of a sense of right and wrong; and confident in his ability to differentiate when he observed behavior or heard opinions. To the coach, the world around him was either white or black. There was no middle ground. He put a high value on dedication, purpose, and hard work. While not all of his teams turned out that way, they all tried hard. Plenty of time on the bench was the reward for anyone who felt differently or who expressed different thoughts. Football was his universe, and his actions and decisions reflected that. He was an autocrat in everything he said.

Indiana was solidly Republican, especially in Putnam, Conway, which was located near the middle of the state and supported itself by agriculture and some manufacturing in areas within the bigger towns, of which there were few. The voters in the area were no-nonsense, down-to-earth, disciplined people who embraced everything that was said by a man like Tommy Mont. Besides, he was a football coach and exuded an aura of toughness in his appearance and his speech, particularly when dealing with people who did not see things the way he did, of which there were a goodly number in a university town like Greencastle. He often referred to those of a liberal viewpoint in his speeches to his team, to the student body, and to the press as "the geniuses," as if everyone knew who he was talking about—and they did.

In short, Tommy Mont was a very good prospect to be a candidate. He was not only strong, he was also smart, and while he couldn't come across as a regular guy (as no coach could), he was liked and respected by everyone.

The announcement had an immediate impact on the team. While Mack, Fox, and the other juniors on the team kind of got a kick out of it and sort of liked the idea, it didn't affect them because, even if our coach won, it wouldn't be in effect until the end of the fall season in 1964. They would graduate the next spring and would not experience the changes brought about by a new coach. Not so with the underclassmen. The worry and anxiety immediately took root in them. After all, they had been recruited by Coach Mont; they had been told by him when he thought they would fix in, and they had received candid assurances of where he thought their career paths would probably lead them after their four years of DePauw football. If the coach went to Congress, all of what they had been told would go out the window and would be subject to a do-over by the next coach, who would have free reign over the personnel in his system. One man's all-American could be another man's third-strong benchwarmer. Well, it was probably not that extreme, but the fact was that with the exception of clear superstars, most players, depending on the coach's personal evaluations, could easily fall anywhere on the depth chart for the team. While the juniors and the seniors knew where they fit in on Coach Mont's team, and had occupied it or had long since left the team, the freshmen and the sophomores knew they were constantly reevaluated and were worried about how they would fit in by their junior year, when the good players could expect to see meaningful playing time. If a proposed career path on a team was disrupted for a player, as was a distinct possibility with a new coach, expectations and all the hard work of fitting in could suddenly be dashed, which would be a disaster for the young players who had made football such an important part of their lives. And for those who would consider the extreme step of transferring to another program, the year of ineligibility they would experience in a transfer (by reason of NCAA rules) and the prohibitive cost of making up lost credits in a transfer from one school to another made transferring an extremely unlikely solution to the situation. The net result for most of the players, including the upperclassmen whose careers would not be so much affected, was that they did not want to see the coach go to Congress, not only because of the uncertain impact it might have on their careers, but also because they liked him as a coach and as a leader.

Coach Mont was conservative and was a disciplinarian, and he had good credentials for a Republican candidate in rural Indiana, but as a college football coach, he had a certain macho attractiveness in the eyes of many voters who had grown up respecting or even idolizing athletes and the men who coached them, like Tommy Mont. His most formidable opponent would be Ralph Mille, the president of the local bank and a seasoned local politician with a number of significant connections he had built over the years. It would be an interesting primary.

The coach had sought the half of his players as much as he could in his efforts just to do the things they could do, like wearing "Coach Mont for Congress" buttons wherever they went, and passing out brochures and pamphlets around campus and in town in their free time. Nobody objected, and most everyone accepted the coaches requests without objection. The campaign was pretty lively, and it culminated at several polling places around Greencastle on primary election day. The coach had asked me and Fox to pass out buttons and pamphlets at the Putnam Conway Fairgrounds, one of the polling places, from 6 p.m. until 10 a.m., primarily because he knew that I had a car and could easily drive us out to the fairgrounds. Without hesitation, Fox and I accepted. The night before the primary, the coach came over to their apartment with a couple of boxes of buttons and pamphlets. He told us exactly where he wanted us to station ourselves upon entry to the fair rounds, and he told us that he would come by around 8 a.m. with a new supply of campaign materials, if they were needed, and some coffee and doughnuts for us. He suggested we go to bed early (which rarely has a bad effect on college-age kids, and wouldn't have in this case).

The alarm went off at 5:00 a.m., quite loudly and rudely. I immediately regretted I had not gone to bed earlier the night before. At 5:00 a.m., there was no way to ease out of bed, it was too risky that I would fall back into a deep sleep while arising slowly, which could be disastrous. I gathered my resolve and willed myself to jump out of bed in the dark. In the process, I knocked the glass containing the unconsumed beer from last night off the nightstand next to my bed. At least it was plastic so, thanks to my planning abilities, it didn't clatter to the wooden floor and reverberate throughout the apartment. I stumbled into the next room and muttered to Fox, "Time to get up and go out to the fairgrounds to spread the good word about the coach."

Fox was not a heavy sleeper and was in sort of a twilight stage. "OK," was all he said as he started to maneuver his 235 pounds out of bed. Fifteen minutes later, both Fox and I were in the hallway, ready for the fifteen-minute drive out to the fairgrounds. We would be out there by 5:45 a.m., give or take five minutes. Just as we had planned. As we got to my Volkswagen, which was parked behind the garage at the end of the driveway, we realized that at this time of year, there was a glaze of ice built up on the windshield, something that we were not used to seeing; but on the other hand, we were not used to starting the car at 5:30 a.m., as we were doing that day. As I started the car and turned the heater up to 80°F and opened the air vents, Fox, who was very resourceful, grabbed the sleeves of his wool coat and ran them briskly and forcefully over the ice-covered windshield, removing most of the glaze on the car. "Now we are clicking!" I exclaimed. "Off we go to the fairgrounds," I shouted from behind the wheel.

There was no traffic on the road at this early hour, so my car rolled into the fairgrounds at 5:50 carrying me, Fox, and all of the coach's campaign literature. Fortunately, there was a streetlight next to the entry driveway of the fairgrounds, so we did not miss our turn. We pulled in and elected to park on the gravel parking lot in a spot located next to the sidewalk that led from the parking lot to the main building, where the booths would be utilized during the day.

"Great spot," I exclaimed. "We can each stand on opposite sides of the sidewalk, greet the voters and pass out the stickers.

"Yeah, nice idea," Fox shot back. "We'll have them covered every way."

We were quite proud of ourselves and our ingenuity. We laid the campaign materials out in the back seat, where we could replenish the materials we were holding in our hands, as the day passed by.

At 6:05, the first vehicle pulled into the parking lot. It was an old pickup truck with a lot of wear and tear. Out popped the single occupant, a man dressed in overalls with a wool billed cap perched on his head. As we greeted the approaching voter, he announced that he owned a farm a couple of miles down the road and was taking a break from his day, that had already been going on for a couple of hours, in order to cast his vote. When he asked for the Republican ballot, Fox and I got excited.

"So good of you to come out, sir," I started out. "I am Charlie Byrum, and this is Bill Fox. We are football players at DePauw, and we were to give you some materials that tell you about our coach, Tommy Mont, who is running for Congress. You are here to vote, and probably have decided what you are going to do with your ballot, but in case you haven't, you can take a minute to look at these materials before you vote, or you can pass them on to friends or family who will vote later today." (Fat chance he would look on them now. But what else could I say on election day itself?)

I extended the materials to the man, who reluctantly took them then proceeded to the building where the voting booths were located, and cast his vote.

Fox and I were still staring at their posts at the sidewalk from the parking lot when the man returned. No one had come in the meantime, and we were starting to feel the effect of the chilly spring morning.

As the man walked by (he had not responded with his name when Fox and I had introduced ourselves), he stopped by us and said, "You know, boys, I admire your coach and how he runs his team. He has the least amount of talent on his team of any school in the conference, but he develops it into a competitive bunch every year, and I know that the players almost all graduate and go on to have productive lives." Fox and I nodded and were ready to respond when the man continued. "I voted for the banker, and I'll tell you why. He is connected, he is part of a political organization, and he can probably do more for us in Washington, if he is elected, than a college football coach; even though, in my opinion, congressmen are only there to get in on something for themselves and don't give a hoot about their constituency. If the banker wins and leaves town, nobody will care. Bankers and politicians are instantly replaceable. Football coaches, on the other hand—particularly good ones, like Tommy Mont—are a different story. They are hard to find and hard to keep. He does a good thing for the school and a good thing for the community. Why would he want to give this up and join the ranks of the crooks and bloodsuckers in Washington who don't do anything for anybody? And if he is crazy enough to want to, why would the voters want to see it happen? You've got a good man there, and he should stay right where he is, doing the most good. Let him get this political itch out of his system and get back to what he does best: coach football."

Fox and I looked at each other. There was nothing we could say. The man was right, but Coach Mont had asked us for our help, so we had given in. "Thanks for coming out. No matter how you voted, the important thing is that you voted." We really meant what we said.

"Thank you, boys. It's good to see about your coach! Players will do for him all that they have the loyalty it takes to do. He is lucky, and you are lucky. I hope the banker wins and coach stays. By the way, my name is Bill Wallace. I'm sorry I didn't introduce myself earlier." He quickly turned and got back into his truck, leaving to resume his workday.

I turned and said to Fox, "You know he is right, don't you?"

There was a quick response from Fox. "Yes, he is; he really is."

As the morning progressed, voters only showed up every fifteen minutes or so, not a lot of traffic. Fox soon came up with the idea that only one of us needed to stand outside the car to meet voters. The others could sit in the car and stay warm. We could alternate. This worked very effectively for a while. After a while, I improved the plan. We could both sit in the car at the same time while enjoying the warmth of the heater. We would take turns getting out of the warm car to greet new voters as they came in.

"You know, Charlie, I think that once we get out of college and into the business world, we will have many moments like this. You start with an idea, improvise, adjust, and further improve upon it as you go along. Eventually, you arrive at perfection. That's what you call business planning." The words had come out like Fox knew what he was talking about.

"Yeah," I responded, "but what we did was find ways to work less and sit in the car more, just enjoying the heater. That's not very industrious."

"Well." Fox blinked. "Progress is taking the situation you are presented with, and making it better. Regardless of the situation, I'll take it. I like the accomplishment," Fox responded.

"I suppose you are right. We didn't make a breakthrough in business or industry, but we found a way to stay warm," I conceded as I leaned back to rest.

It was almost 9:00. Four hours had transpired since we first woke up, and we had spent more than half of those hours in the cold. Fox was tired.

I suddenly woke up as the glimmer of the sun off the roof of an approaching car reached my eyes. I looked at my watch. "Holy cripes. It's ten o'clock," I exclaimed. "Coach Mont will be here with coffee and doughnuts any minute, and we've been sleeping for an hour."

Fox heard me loud and clear. We quickly scrambled to wipe the sleep out of our eyes and jumped out of the car, each loaded with a good supply of bumper stickers and campaign buttons. It was none too soon. I slammed the door shut as he made his exit for the car, he spotted Coach Mont's station wagon turning into the driveway of the fairgrounds.

"Lucky break!" I shouted over to Fox. "If coach had found us asleep on the job, our futures on the team would not be very pretty."

Fox just shrugged his shoulders. Maybe there had been more truth in my words than I'd first thought. At least I would never find out. We greeted our coach with a glowing report that even though the turnout had been light, all the voters had gladly accepted the buttons and bumper stickers, and Fox and I had spoken about him in glowing terms. We would never know how many. All we knew was that we had dodged a bullet and had fulfilled our promise to the coach (well, sort of).

As it turned out, the fates and the voters overwhelmingly decided that Coach Mont could best serve the community by staying on as a university football coach. The banker won the primary by a two-to-one margin and became the Republican nominee and eventually the winner of the district and would serve several terms. Everyone associated with DePauw football—the players, the students, the parents, and the administration—was silently relieved with the outcome of the election, and life went on in Greencastle.

CHAPTER 36

RENE BREAKS HIS WRIST

THE 1964 GAME AT EVANSVILLE was a tough one for the Tigers. First, we lost the game against Evansville on their home field, due in large part to the performance of an Evansville defensive end named Marty Amsler, who was dominant throughout the game. He constantly stiffed out inside running plays at the line and chased down our outside plays with speed and ease. This resulted in a sizable loss for us on the road, and a costly injury to us, which resulted in the loss of our left halfback, Rene Bichet, through a broken wrist. Rene was the starter that day, and I was his backup. He was five feet nine inches tall and weighed 180 pounds, and he was more of a power runner than me, but I was slightly faster. He was from McKees Rocks, Pennsylvania, and he was as tough as they come, as are many players from Pennsylvania. He was an excellent blocker and had nifty moves, and it took a lot to get him down.

When he carried the ball, he had this uncanny ability to coil as he was running with the ball and then unload into any unsuspecting player who was doing in to tackle him. Rene's only shortcoming was that he had stone hands and could not be counted on as a receiver. Try as he might to improve, he just didn't have the touch to catch a football that was thrown to him, so the quarterback rarely did. In the big scheme of things for the DePauw offense, it didn't make much difference anyhow, because the

DePauw offense didn't throw the ball that much, so his shortcomings weren't obvious. It was always a pleasure to watch Rene execute the Power Six in a game. The play involved Rene moving to right halfback, then going out to block the defensive end. Alcott, the fullback, would take the ball and cut behind Rene's back. Usually, the play gained at least five yards since Rene would knock the defensive end to the ground. The play was prominent in the DePauw playbook.

Things suddenly went bad for Rene and the Tigers about midway through the third quarter of the Evansville game. Rene ran an off-tackle play and stuck his hand out to break his fall as he was topped up at the line. He immediately got up and ran to the sideline as injured players are taught to do, clutching his wrist. When Coach Mont saw this, he suspected what had happened and yelled at the top of his lungs, "Charlie, get in there for Rene." In that moment, while I ran in to take over left halfback, the team's doctor took Rene to the bench and started to look over his wrist, shaking his head.

"He's done," said the Doc.

It was second down and eight yards to go for a first down when I entered the game for Rene. By that time, the Evansville pass rush had become so fierce that Coach Mont had decided not to risk giving up the ball on an interception or a sack, so he resorted to a short running game just to buy some time to get to the end of the first half when the Tigers could go in and make some adjustments. As instructed, Bruce Mackey, the Tiger quarterback, called two straight running plays where the ball would be handed to the left halfback who would run off-tackle. This time, it would be me, not Rene, who would get the ball.

On the first play, the Evansville linebacker shot into the gap where the play was designed to go, and I ran into him for no gain. On the second play, the Tiger offensive tackle, Mark Moore, threw a very good block, and I broke through for a five-yard gain, but Amsler (who had beaten the Tiger tackle on the other side) ran down the line and hit me from the side with full force. I didn't know what it was like to be hit by a truck, but I concluded the blindside hit I received from Amsler would be something like it. *What an animal*, I thought to myself as I turned off the field as the punting team trotted in. As things turned out, Amsler, who would graduate that year, would later sign with the Chicago Bears and have a nice five-year career with them.

After a punt by DePauw, I got back to the bench and ran over to Rene, who looked like he had tears in his eyes. "What did the doctor say?" I asked immediately.

"He said it looks like a break, but he can't be sure without X-rays. I'll have them Monday morning back at Putnam Conway General in Greencastle," Rene replied in a dejected voice. "It looks like you are going to have to carry the load, Charlie."

I wasn't worried about having to be the first team left halfback for the balance of this game, or more games, for that matter. This was what I had prepared for all year. But what bothered me right then was that it looked like this might be the end for Rene, who was my friend. Rene had never missed a practice, as far as anyone could remember. He had been a hard worker and worked relentlessly to improve his game and his skills. He was very popular and was liked by everyone on the team. Rene was an art major and was good friends with my fraternity brother John Barry and would come over to the Phi Delta Theta house just to pass the time. I was very upset with the idea that if Rene's wrist was broken, it meant the end of his career, just when he was getting his big chance after so much waiting. In addition, a break would have an effect on the ability of Rene, who was right-handed, to paint, which he did a lot of as an art major. For the rest of the game and over the weekend, while waiting for Rene's X-rays to be performed, I thought very little about what the injury would mean for my own career.

At practice on Monday, Coach Mont announced—with Rene at his side, dressed in street clothes and with a cast on his hand and a dejected look on his face—that Rene's wrist was not only broken, it was fractured, and he would be out for the season. There was not much reaction from the team, since most of them had suspected this since Saturday and were prepared for it. This is football. Everyone gets hurt at some time in their career, and when they do, you better have someone else ready.

Before the team broke up for drills, Coach Mont looked me in the eyes and announced, "Charlie, you go over and practice with the first team." And then he said to Mike Burns, who also played defense, "Mike, you go over and play with the second team." Mike would take my old spot.

It was over just like that. Rene, to his credit, would show up to every practice until the end of the year and would come to all of the games, doing whatever he could to help out and encourage the team. He was that kind of guy. I was sure Rene thought from time to time about what might have been, but he never showed it.

In the meantime, it was just starting to sink in with me that my football career had changed dramatically. I was a starter, and I had better be prepared for it.

CHAPTER 37

REUTER'S RAIDERS

Small-college football presents a number of problems to coaches of the schools that play the game that are not present in the big schools. One of the biggest problems is how and when he uses the players who do not play much. In the small college teams, unlike the schools from the large conferences, there are fewer good players to put in there after a team's best players are put in by the coach. After the first-string is taken out of the game, the players left on the bench are not so good and should not be playing who the first-string is playing. They are not good enough to be playing at any level because the other team's players will beat them, no matter who is on the bench. The coach with a weak second-string can't beat anybody because he does not have the players to do it, so then as always a group suiting up but not expecting to play in the actual game. Generally, these players are just glad to be on their school's team, are happy the sit on the bench, and are satisfied with whatever playing time their coach gives them. During the course of a football season, these players still perform functions that are useful to the team if it is to have any chance of success over the season. This team is always one injury away from losing an important player. A replacement player (or players) is essential, even if they are not good enough to beat out a starter, as long as they know how to execute the plays followed by the team. These fringe players have gone through the playbooks; participated in the conditioning, scrimmages, and chalk talks all year, and have worked as much as the starters. They are game-ready and have put in the time and effort to get there. It could be said that their commitment to the team is greater than that of the starter, since the team benefits from their hard work, but they should not be put in the game. Everybody knows it. The fringe players will only play if their team does not have enough players to put in the game; but without them, there would be no team.

Coach Mont knew this and decided during the week of the Tigers' game with Valparaiso to field a kickoff team comprised of fringe players to kick the ball off whenever it was DePauw's turn to do so. The coach designated Fritz Stresen Reuter, a junior from Bloomfield Hills, Michigan, as its captain. Fritz had not gone out for football until his junior year because he had made the decision to concentrate exclusively on his grades when he'd enrolled in college, despite the fact that he'd played the sport all four years when he was in high school. He was a strong-looking player and was very fast and very popular. The players had formed the opinion that Fritz might well be a starting player now, had he played his freshman and sophomore years. He spent the week looking at films of the Valparaiso team and examining how they lined up to run the returns to the left, to the right, and up the middle. He also noted which backs in Valparaiso were involved in the returns at various times. He called his team Reuter's Raiders.

Fritz went out to the center of the field when it was time for the coin toss between the teams, and he called heads when the coin was in the air. The captains of the two teams shook hands and retreated to the sidelines. Reuter's Raiders lined up in formation to kick off. As the whistle blew, the DePauw kicker approached the ball and gave it a mighty kick.

The Valparaiso kick returns weaved through the Raiders and scored with ease. Then, when Valparaiso kicked off, DePauw fumbled Valparaiso's kickoff, and Valparaiso picked up the ball and scored again with ease. As Valparaiso rejoiced, Fritz quickly looked for a place to hide.

"Alright, Raiders. Let's hit 'em hard now and show them the last kickoff was a fluke," Fritz shouted at the top of his lungs. The Raiders grunted back in unison, and they took their positions.

I thought to myself, *That last Valparaiso score just might not have been a fluke. They knew exactly what they were doing.* I crossed my fingers and hoped for the best on this one.

The Raiders lined up to receive another kickoff, knowing they needed to make a better showing than the last time in order for the coach to maintain the confidence he'd had in the group when he'd assembled them. To a man, they all had determined, angry looks on their faces as they waited for the whistle to put the ball in play so DePauw could return the kick. The Valparaiso kicker got his foot into the kick and sent it all the way to the five-yard line. The Raiders charged down the field, whooping and hollering, determined to make amends for their last performance, giving me and the other DePauw players the hope that the Raiders had turned things around, and justifying Coach Mont's bold decision to assemble the group and give them another meaningful assignment. Then, as the kickoff settled into the arms of the Valparaiso return man on his five-yard line, the wheels came off for the Raiders.

First, the two lead tacklers who had charged downfield to stop the return man in his tracks ran right by him without laying a hand on him, and when they turned around to grab him from behind, they got their feet tangled and watched him scamper upfield with fifteen yards of space completely open for him to run into. Next, the Valparaiso onside blockers whose job it was to create a running lane along the right side of the field performed their job flawlessly, and each knocked a Raider down, thus opening the right side running lane free of tacklers. Finally, the DePauw safety man whose job consisted of holding back and putting himself in position to tackle the return man, should he break through the other DePauw tacklers for some unexplained reason, expected the return man to break to the left side and ran over there to cover when the blocking was set up for the runner to cover the right lane, leaving the entire right side of the field clear for the runner who proceeded to run up the right sideline undisturbed and into the DePauw end zone.

Two kickoff opportunities for the Raiders and two disastrous touchdowns. The great Raider experiment of putting in unused players with fresh legs and lots of energy had been a noble idea and had not worked. The looks on the faces of the Raiders as they walked off the field to the end of the bench, when they knew they had not stopped returns very well, told the entire story. From this point on, DePauw's regular kickoff team would cover kicks, but they would not have the opportunity to do so that day because DePauw would not go on to score again way down to the ten-yard line of Valparaiso settled into the hands of the Valparaiso return man before he charged upfield. Not bunch up to tackle the receiver. Suddenly, the two outside men on the blocking line of the Valparaiso receiving team crisscrossed so as to confuse the DePauw players on the outside protection lanes on the field, and they looked up with confusion as the crossing blockers knocked them off their feet. As that happened, the players on the second line of the Valparaiso return team knocked down the next two onside players from DePauw, leaving a twenty-yard gap on the outside of the DePauw kicking team, allowing the Valparaiso return man to take the ball down to the DePauw thirty before the Valparaiso return man was touched. DePauw was shocked and became even more shocked as Valparaiso ran the ball into the DePauw end zone in three more plays.

As the Raiders ran off the field, looks of disappointment showed on their faces. They were done for the day, and probably for the season.

CHAPTER 38

CAMP LEJEUNE

Sometime in the middle of January of my senior year, the athletic director of Washington University in St. Louis called Jim Loveless, the athletic director of DePauw, to announce that he was going to drop the DePauw game that had been scheduled for October 23 in Greencastle, for no explainable reason. It was his prerogative to do so, as it was before February 1, which was the last date when a team could cancel a game with a foe scheduled for the following fall. This was not a frequent occurrence, but it happened from time to time. The reasons required were not always made clear. In the case of Washington University in St. Louis, I suspected (as did most of the Tiger players) that the Washington coach was still peeved about the time when Coach Mont had stalled the beginning of last year's game between the two teams that took place in Greencastle in order to allow Stu Young and Bill Alcott, two of DePauw's best players, to take the premed test on Saturday morning in Indianapolis and hurry back while changing into their uniforms in the car driven by Young's father, in time to start the Washington game about half an hour late.

When the Washington coach realized what had happened to him, he'd promised he would do something about it. This was it. A cancellation this late into the process was hard to recover from, particularly for a game that was to take place on October 23, one of the best weeks in the season when the air was crisp and the leaves had changed color but had not yet fallen from the trees, a perfect football weekend. Now there would be no opponent and no game. The Washington coach had executed his revenge, and it hurt. Coach Mont was bummed. He didn't show it, but his players knew it. What was worse, Washington quickly scheduled a game against a nasty opponent for October 23, which was announced only a week after the DePauw cancellation had been announced. There was no doubt in anyone's mind about what had happened. The Washington coach had executed a well-planned retribution that had caught DePauw by surprise. After a while, everyone had come to accept it and went on with life—everyone but Coach Mont, that is. He felt like he had left the team in a vulnerable position last year with his delaying tactic, and he had to do something to make it up to the team. And he did.

Shortly before the first game of the season in my senior year, Coach Mont made an announcement at a team meeting on a Monday, which was the day the team normally assembled to review game films of the upcoming opponent. On October 23, the Tigers would fly to North Carolina to play the Camp Lejeune Marines. Almost universally, the reaction of the team was to say, "What?" out loud, upon hearing the coach's words.

Coach Mont realized this was a big surprise for his team. They had resigned themselves to taking the weekend of October 23 off and getting a little break from football. While some of them were still a little peeved and perplexed by the prospects of the cancellation, most of the team had accepted it and were even looking forward to a midseason break. Usually, by the middle of October, there were a number of injuries sustained by the players that, while not disabling, were significant enough to benefit from a one-week break that would allow for some healing time. For those who were not injured, almost everyone had little nicks, bruises, and pulls that could improve with a little break from the schedule. As a result, the team was looking forward to the time off, primarily because there was no other alternative. And now this announcement from the coach. Marines playing football? Where? How big were they? How old were they? Who did they play? Dozens of questions popped into the minds of the players as the coach announced the news. Coach knew he had to be comprehensive in explaining things.

Camp Lejeune was a US Marine Corps base camp located in Jacksonville, North Carolina. It was a huge operation with a population of over 33,000 people, including active-duty, retired, and civilian employees and their dependents who were located on the base and in the surrounding community. Its main purpose was to serve as a home base to train, equip, and house military-ready marines and associated support personnel and their families. The biggest nearby major city was Raleigh, and the closest airport was in Richards, North Carolina, about thirty-five miles from the facility. Camp Lejeune contained not only the training and support systems for soldiers who were ready for battle, but it also had housing, offices, storage, and commercial and government spaces. And it had hospitals, schools, movie theaters, parks, and everything a significant-size city would be expected to have, just like similar camps such as Quantico, Camp Pendleton, Parris Island, and dozens of others in the US, and in some cases, out of the country.

Each camp had its own football team with full-time coaches and full-time teams who played each other throughout the season in many sports. Football was just one of them. The players were men who had enlisted in the marine corps and had tried out for the team. If a player was chosen, football was about the only activity he would be assigned to while in the service, so long as he was good enough to play. While teams were comprised of those who tried out for them, no matter what the age, a large percentage of the players on a base team were former high school players who had not gone on to play in college, for their own reasons, while an equally large percentage were former college players who were now spending their time in the service and were able to put this experience and training to use as masters of the base team. This was not unique to the marines, and it took place in all branches of the service.

The Camp Lejeune Marines traditionally had one of the strongest service teams on a regular base, and it had a constant influx of talent from college conferences, particularly the Southeastern Conference and the Atlantic Coast Conference, which were comprised of schools in nearby states. My teammates and I would go on to learn that the Lejeune team drew approximately 30 percent of its players from the Southeastern Conference and about 20 percent from the Atlantic Coast Conference. These players had graduated from those schools and had put in enough time to develop the skills to be good. Moreover, while a number of the players were the same ages as the college boys on the Tigers, most of them were two to four years older and had achieved a greater level of physical maturity than me and my teammates. We would later find out the starting fullback for the Camp Lejeune team was a behemoth named Patsy Strano, who had been the starting fullback for the University of Mississippi the year before. Strano's playing weight at Mississippi had been 225 pounds, but for the Camp Lejeune team, he now tipped the scales at 250 pounds. The biggest players on the Tigers were their offensive tackles (Fox and Mark Moore) and their defensive tackle (Ed Gardner), all in the range of 235 pounds. The weights of linemen for the Camp Lejeune team were well in the ranges of Strano, being between 250 to 280 pounds, with most of them coming from highly competitive college conferences. Had Coach Mont given the Tigers this information when he explained the opportunity to play the marines, they may not have decided to go, but at least they would have thought long and hard about it. No one on suspected that the coach would have fudged information about the size and makeup of the Camp Lejeune team. They preferred to believe he had not been informed when the arrangements for the game had been made.

The game between the Tigers and the marines came about through the effort of John Kellogg, who had been a safety at DePauw about five years ago. He had been a good player for the Tigers, and his value to the team had been through the toughness and discipline he'd demonstrated on the field. These were traits that served him well as a football player and made him well-suited for success in the marines, which he experienced in a big way. Kellogg didn't play football as a marine because he had too many military and administrative responsibilities, but he still loved the game, as most Tigers would have after their playing days were over. Moreover, he had kept in touch with the DePauw coaches, who pretty much were all there during his playing days, particularly Ted Kadala, the defense coordinator. He learned of DePauw's plight not the cana??? of the Washington University in St. Louis game hour long after it was announced. After determining with the Camp Lejeune football coaching staff and the marine brass that scheduling the Tigers would be fine with them, he called Coach Mont, and the agreement to play was readily reached. The coach quickly got the approval of the DePauw athletic director and the university president, and the game was set. No one knew for sure which approval had to be obtained from the NCAA for the game to be played or if so, which it was obtained.

The first thing the players wanted to know when the coach told them about the game was how they would get there. The games the Tigers had played were always in Indiana and the surrounding states, including Illinois, Michigan, Kentucky, and Ohio, and occasionally in Missouri and Wisconsin, and the mode of transportation was always by bus. The trip to North Carolina, announced the coach, would be made by airplane.

Nervous laughter with a touch of apprehension was emitted by the team as the logistics were announced. It was 1964. DePauw was a small school in Indiana, comprised of a good number of students from small Midwestern towns. Moreover, many of the families sending their kids there faced many struggles just to keep their kids in school. Flying in a commercial airplane was just not a common experience for the players in the room and their families. My assessment was that less than half the people in the room had flown before, and those who had flown had only done it once or twice. I had not flown, even though my dad made a good living, so this would be a new experience for me as well. I was getting all pumped up for the experience, even though the game was several months away. *Wow,* I thought to myself, *flying halfway across the country to play a team of former big-time college players, and staying on a marine base all weekend, to boot. It's almost as exciting as a bowl game.* I had just heard the part about staying on the marine base from my coach, and I really was not sure about that part. I told my parents exactly that when I told them what was to happen. "Don't worry about it," said my father upon hearing the news of the trip. "I was in the air force during World War II and was stationed at Fort Sam Houston in Texas. I had a heck of a time back then. You will, too."

I was not so sure. The United States was involved in a conflict in Vietnam that was escalating. Americans were getting shit, and there was talk of escalation of hostilities. The idea of anything military spooked me a little bit, even if it was for a football game.

It was the practice of the DePauw coaching staff not to get too far ahead of itself in preparing for the upcoming game each week. Mondays were devoted to watching films for the Saturday game that had been completed a couple of days ago. Sometimes they were good, and sometimes not. Each player examined the Monday film sessions to see how the recently played game had been handled by the team. The coaches focused on the score and how the team had performed. Every player, however, was very interested in how the films showed the way he'd played personally since the film results would certainly impact the coaches' assessments of him and could affect some decisions on playing time. Films of the next week's appointment, which were shown on Tuesday, didn't usually draw much interest from the team. This was when the coach showed the film of the game last week between the Lejeune Marines and Quantico.

"No wonder he held off on showing us this," Mark said when he saw just the first few minutes. "The Lejeune players are big, brutal, and nasty, and we have to play them in five days on their field. Lord, help us."

The silence that suddenly took over the DePauw film room was a good indication that the same conclusion had occurred instantaneously to the entire Tiger team.

Coach Mont let a few more plays flash on the screen before he spoke. The last one was on where Quantico's halfback ran a simple off-tackle play on the right end and was promptly flattened by the huge charging Lejeune middle linebacker who knew exactly where the play was going. It wasn't the speed of the Lejeune team that impressed me and the Tigers so much, it was about the same as they got from most of their opponents. It was the sheer size of the Lejeune players. To a man, they were just plain huge. What was more, they hit, very hard, whether they were blocking or tackling. Part of it was their size, which was clearly superior to Quantico's, but the rest was the ferocity with which they made contact and sustained it on either side of the line of scrimmage. Once a Quantico player and a Lejeune player engaged, the Quantico player was usually stood up or driven back. It was quite a display. Coach Mont wanted to create respect in his players for the Lejeune team, but he didn't want to discourage them, which was what he would have done had he made them watch the game film for too long. He turned the film projector off after the first quarter. Still, the DePauw players had become very silent.

Coach Mont stepped up to the front of the room. "Gentlemen, this is a good team you will be playing, but they have been beaten twice this year. They can—and have—been beaten."

Yeah, I thought, *a bunch of twenty-five-year-old ex-major college players beaten by another band of twenty-five-year-old ex-college players. Big deal. Where do we fit in to this equation? All these guys.*

"You will have to play a very good game if you are going to beat this team. You are as good as they are. I know it. I would not have scheduled this game if I thought otherwise. Does anyone want me to back out? I will contact Captain Kellogg and call this off. I'll be glad to do it. The marines have a little more experience and a little more size than you, but this team—your team—has heart and fears mostly, so what do you want to do?"

Ed Gardner, one of the captains, but a man of few words, who had been voted in because of his toughness and effort on the field, stood up and addressed the coach and the team. "Coach, we had the opportunity to play taken from us, and have wanted to do something about it. You did your part. You found a team for us to play. Now we have to do our part and beat them. I can't wait to get off the plane and take the word to them."

He meant it. This was Ed Gardner. He wasn't afraid of any situation or anybody.

Mark Moore, one of the big tacklers, shouted out, "Let's get 'em!"

And pretty soon, the whole team was on its feet, yelling, "Get 'em now, right now!" and quickly left the room to dress for practice. On my way out of the room, I cast a look as Coach Mont, who had a very proud look on his face.

That Friday, the Tigers, with their equipment bags, took a couple of university buses on the one-and-a-half-hour drive to the Indianapolis International Airport and boarded the plane for Raleigh, North Carolina. While about fifteen members of the team had flown on a commercial airline, the balance had not. It was 1964, and flying was not an experience that many people had gone through, and those who had had flown only once or twice. This fact accounted, in large part, for a very nervous state of mind for the Tiger team. There was plenty of laughter and banter, of course, the type that always occurs where a group of people is about to embark on an unusual experience they were not accustomed to, but it had more than a little tone of anxiety to it. After all, most of the players had never been higher from the ground than the twentieth floor of a city office building, and soon, they would be hurtling over the earth, thousands of feet above it. It was not lost on them, and it showed in their faces. Here they were, a bunch of well-conditioned, athletic kids, accustomed to spending two and a half hours on a Saturday running full speed into other football players in a state of bedlam with serious injury a distinct possibility, looking like a bunch of small children creeping in a state of terror to their first day of school.

The laughter and banter stopped entirely as they walked out the doors of the hangar and saw the sixty-seat propeller plane sitting on the tarmac. They were aware that once they boarded and fastened their seat belts, it would just be a few minutes before the university they had come from, the city of Indianapolis, and the whole world as they knew it would become speed on the earth. Resigned to the fact that there was no option other than to complete their journey, the Tigers silently ascended the stairs on the runway that led to the plane, took their seats, and buckled up for the three-hour trip to North Carolina. As the propellers started up and roared to a full crescendo, many silently said little prayers, and as the plane lifted off the runway, a few of them shut their eyes tightly. Soon, however, the team was hurtling through the sky and knifing through the clouds that until now most of them had only observed from the ground. It was magical and exhilarating, and their fear and trepidation soon made way for amazement. In the future, most of them would fly on a regular basis routinely. While a lot of them would forget this initial experience on an airplane, many would not.

As the plane touched down on the runway to the Raleigh-Durham International Airport, the Tigers looked out the windows at the gently rolling hills and the cluster of southern pine trees, and they realized they were no longer in the flat agricultural expanses of Indiana. As they descended the stairs from the plane that had been rolled up to meet them, they were struck by the gentle, moist wind that carried the scent of pines that were prevalent in the area. *Even the airport is different*, I thought. I was very favorably impressed.

As they emerged for the baggage area with their equipment bags, they spotted the military bases that had been sent to the airport to Camp Lejeune. They all noticed when a very fit-looking marine corporal in his late twenties walked briskly up to Coach Mont and extended his hand, which the coach quickly accepted and shook heartily. Jim Kellogg had been an all-conference halfback nearly a decade ago at DePauw and looked like he could still play. The two men spoke briefly, both with wide grins on their faces, until Coach Mont had to break away to get his charges on the buses that had arrived. Mack knew that Coach Mont and Kellogg had a lot of catching up to do and would probably do so late that night over a couple of beers, after the Tiger team turned in. As the coach boarded the bus, he was smiling broadly as he took his seat. Why wouldn't he? One of the benefits of coaching at the college level was that it was an opportunity to help mold young lives into who they would eventually become, and to be a part of the experiences players go through in the process. A person like Corporal Kellogg, who had been an athlete and a student of high caliber at DePauw, had continued with exemplary service to his company and was the kind of person anyone would have wanted to take credit for helping him along the way. He was a sterling example of what the current group of young Tigers would want to aspire to become.

The buses entered the base and drove along a tree-lined road for about two miles before they stopped at several large, wood-frame buildings housing the barracks. The Tigers were broken up into small groups to bunk together in designated areas. The groups were based on positions, with four or five players in each group. My group consisted of the four players who were halfbacks on offense. The idea was that, by having players who played the same position bunk together, they would talk about plays and assignments and would be in a state of readiness concerning their positions by the day of the game. It was a nice idea, but not a realistic one. The last thing a group of football players talked about when they were together were the plays they would run. It just wasn't interesting. In my group, the banter ran from what freshman girls were the most developed to the best-lasting beers, and it went south from there. Moreover, these groups were not assigned to individual dorm-type rooms but to a large barracks area with all of the beds lined up side by side in a great hall under one roof. In that kind of situation, players gravitated to what they felt were the most interesting discussions, not to the ones concerning the plays they would run.

After they unpacked their bags and put their containers in the footlockers assigned to the beds, they lined up and proceeded to the mess hall for dinner. As we walked to the mess hall, I noted that we were the only group walking heavily, each at their own pace. The other groups, all uniformed, were walking in an organized, regimental manner, all in synchronized step with each member of the group intently staring forward.

Actually, it's kind of creepy, I thought. *Not what I'm used to. It's very structured, with no spontaneity, even in their most leisurely manner. What's more*, I thought, *these guys are likely to be shot at before this is all over for them.* The US was in a conflict in Vietnam, and more and more soldiers were being sent over there each week. In 1964, the conflict was escalating, and more and more US troops were deployed in combat. Not a very enviable position. More and more members of the armed services were being supplied via the draft, which was an unpleasant process for college-age students. The members of the Tigers were all deferred for the draft because they were students, but that was not guaranteed to last forever. It was a pretty glum situation. I didn't know how many occupants of the base would eventually be directly involved in the conflict, but it was unsettling.

As dawn broke on Saturday morning, the day of the game, the team was in the mess hall to get breakfast just as they had done for dinner the night before. They got their individual trays and lined up to choose their food. The marines, with expressionless faces, sort of slopped something on their plates. I had never eaten at a four-star restaurant at this point in my life, but I was certain that when I did, it would not be like this.

The Tigers was back to the barracks after breakfast to relax and get taped for the game. Some took showers, but others waited, since they would have to take another shower after the game, and why do it twice? They all had to take a trip to the latrine at some point after breakfast, due to all the coffee they had consumed. The latrine consisted of six toilets on one side of the room facing six more on the other side. It was not a pretty sight to sit on a toilet where your only choice was to watch people to your left, your right, or straight ahead who were crapping. It was at this moment that I realized that, all things being equal, life in the armed services, even a short part of it, was not for me. I just wanted to play the game, get on the plane, and go home. I was sure a lot of my teammates felt the same way.

The Tigers dressed in the barracks for the game and hopped on the buses that would take them to the stadium at 11:00 a.m. when they would warm up, have a chalk talk, and take the field for a 1:00 p.m. kickoff.

The trip to the stadium was about fifteen minutes. It was on the outskirts of the fort. It was a funtimed looking brick facade that probably had a seating capacity of about ten thousand. I had no idea how many people actually attended the average Lejeune football game, but I guessed probably a lot because football has sort of a military beat to it, and because there was probably not much else to do. As we got off the base, the humid air and the pine scent manifested again, and I breathed it in. It was probably the best part of the trip for me. The area was beautiful, even parts of the base.

The Tigers would walk the field to warm up. They were doing calisthenics in the end zone with the direction of their captains, Ed Gardner and Tom Cooper, when the Lejeune team came charging out of their dressing area and onto the field. They were pretty charged up, probably at the idea of playing some college boys who they saw as rich and spoiled (at least as far as they were concerned), and they were whooping it up as they ran quickly to field. The Tigers stopped their calisthenics for a brief moment and stared. This was something you did not want to do before a game, because it can betray a feeling of surprise, amazement, and worst of all, apprehension. But the Tigers stared, and why wouldn't they? The Lejeune team was big; no, it was huge. The players were all around twenty-two to twenty-five years of age, about four years older than the Tigers. A lot can happen in four years, certainly the addition of weight and maturity. Both of these were present in abundance. Thank goodness Coach Mont had elected for the Tigers to hear them which game shirts and pants for the game. This makes a player look bigger, so the Tigers had that advantage, not that the marines cared, but they had worn their red jerseys and black pants, so at least they didn't look as big as they would have in white. But big they looked, and big they were.

Members of a military base football team don't do much during their time in the service but train for football. They work out, run plays, study playbacks, and play football. There is little beyond that. This is the reason that so many recruits opt to try out for the football team. It's a good life, the duty is not so hard, and they are kept out of harm's way.

The night before the game, Colonel Kellogg dropped off some game programs for the Tiger team so that they had souvenirs of the experience. I grabbed one and sat around looking at it with my teammates. In it, the members of the Lejeune team were listed, along with their colleges, their positions, and their weights and heights. Most of them had played on teams in the Atlantic Coast Conference and the Southeastern Conference, not surprising, given the locals of Camp Lejeune. Much of my teammates recognized a few of the names and remembered they'd watched a lot of them play on TV back when the members of the Tigers had been in high school. Patsy Strano, the fullback from Mississippi, was one of them. When he was at Ole Miss, he was about 220 pounds, which was big for college. Now he was listed at 250 pounds, a lot bigger than DePauw's two biggest players, Fox and Ed Gardner, who were listed at 255 pounds. The Lejeune linemen were even bigger, all between 240 and 260 pounds.

When the coin toss took place, the Tigers elected to receive, having won the toss. The captains shook hands and returned to their respective teams.

I noted that as the kickoff approached, the whooping and hollering of the Lejeune team stopped and they got around to taking care of business. Very military. Take care of the task at hand and don't give in to distraction.

I was one of the return men on the kickoff. As the referee's whistle blew and the ball flew into the air, I saw it was coming to me. *Well,* I thought, *I might as well be the first to see what these guys are about. Someone has to.*

As the ball settled into my arms at around the ten-yard line, I ran forward and then broke to the rhythm to pick up the wall that was supposed to form on the right. I got up to about the twenty-two-yard line when the first marine hit me. The hit did not take me down, but it threw me off my stride and left me open for the second hit, which came shortly after the first. It was a hard hit, but like other I had experienced from team like Indiana State and Ball State. As the game went on, the hitting was hard, but less ferocious than DePauw had expected, and probably as ferocious as the Lejeune team had expected. It was a well-played game, and the marines—due to their size and the number of fresh bodies they could and did substitute freely during the course of the game—wore the Tigers down and won twenty to six. The only real injury that occurred was to a Lejeune player who took a shot in the ribs from Tim Freemuster, the DePauw sophomore halfback, and had to leave the game.

After they went back to the barracks, showered, and dressed, the Tigers boarded the buses, said goodbye to Corporal Kellogg (who had come to see them off and thank them for coming), and headed back to the airport. They felt good about themselves because they had done a lot better than anyone had expected them to, even themselves. *That's why you have to play the game before you write the story*, I thought. It was a good feeling, all in all, and everyone slept well on the plane ride back to Indiana.

CHAPTER 39

I GET KNOCKED OUT

THE TIGERS TRAVELED TO RENSSELAER, Indiana, which was about two hours north of Greencastle, to play the Pumas of St. Joseph's College, a small, all -male Catholic school of about one thousand graduates. St. Joseph's was the smallest school in the conference, but it had a pretty good tradition and a good turnout for the team, as was generally true for most Catholic schools with football programs. The Pumas were well-coached and in good playing shape, but they had the disadvantage of having teams comprised of smaller players, and as hard as they played—and they did play hard—they lost more games than they won. When you played them, however, you knew you were in a game.

I had my own ideas about why St. Joseph's played so hard and with so much abandon. St. Joseph's was not a coeducational school and was located in a small farming community in Central Indiana. I surmised (and probably correctly) that without girls and without the city lights, it was not a fun place to be, without the normal college-type activities and opportunities. It was not a great place to be stuck in for someone who had expected or hoped for a well-rounded, balanced social situation when he'd enrolled. This probably led to a long-pent-up frustration and angst among the students, and I believed that playing football and having the opportunity to pound and run into someone for three hours on a Saturday afternoon—which football allowed the most physical and aggressive students to do—was probably a very good release. The Pumas always had a full squad and were always very aggressive, so there was probably a lot of truth in what I had surmised.

The contest between the Tigers and the Pumas was hard-fought with the blocking and tackling by both teams being very physical and done with a much higher level of intensity than what I was used to in the conference. The two schools were already out of contention for the conference championship when they met on this crisp, shady afternoon in early October. It obviously meant a lot to both schools to try to prevail over each other because of the potential that the loser of the game might finish in last place in the conference, a distinction that neither wanted.

The St. Joseph's players, as a group, were generally smaller than what the Tigers were used to. This had to be expected from a school of only one thousand students which, unlike Ball State, with an enrollment of eighteen thousand, did not have a huge number of large and professed players. As hard as they played, St. Joseph's never stayed for very long in its games with the likes of Ball State during the years I played in the conference. After receiving the kickoff and four series of downs, Alcott's size started to manifest itself, and he was chewing up big chunks of yardage with every carry against the smaller St. Joseph's players.

While not getting as many carries as Alcott, I was also getting some good yardage on my runs when the ball was handed off to me. DePauw was up twenty-one to nothing at the end of the first half, with one play having hit several times with a great degree of success. It was a play wherein Mackey would stick the ball into the belly of Alcott, who was running into the line as if to go between the hole separating the right guard and the right tackle, but would then pull it out and pitch it back to me, who was circling around back from my left halfback position to take the pitch and run around the right end. In the past plays, the right end had been able to seal off the left outside St. Joseph's linebacker who had instinctively moved toward the center to pursue Alcott when he got the ball. On many of the plays, I gained guard at least eight yards and on me, I gained fifteen yards.

The play had been so successful that Mackey thought it was a good time to try it again, so he called for it. This time, however, the left outside linebacker had anticipated the play and stayed home, refusing to bite on the take handoff to Alcott. This left him outside Earl Liebach, DePauw's right end who could not block him in and search him off from my running road. When I saw the play develop, I shouted past Liebach across the line of scrimmage toward Liebach just as I had taken the pitch and turned upfield. When I first laid eyes in the linebacker, he was going full speed to hit me in my chosen path. My DePauw linemen had obscured my vision of the linebacker, so he was only two steps away from meeting me head-on, too late for me to react when I first saw the linebacker.

The linebacker's helmet hit the side of my helmet with full force upon impact. The difference for the two players was that the linebacker had planned the hit, lined up, and pushed off the ground which forced them to get something extra on the hit just for emphasis while I was totally unsuspecting and had no idea it was coming. There was a resounding collision as the helmets of the two players met.

I had been hit before in games and practices many times, but it had never been like this. My vision was suddenly filled with bright light and then went to darkness. I did not know what had happened, except the next thing I was aware of was that I was laying on the flat of my back. I instinctively rolled over to get on my hands and tried to get to my feet. I managed to do just that, but when I anticipated to stand from the kneeling position, I fell face-forward, and the next thing I remembered was the trainer, Ralph Berlin, sticking a broken capsule of ammonia under my nose to bring me back to consciousness. My head ached and throbbed with a kind of pain I had never experienced before. After some more offs by Ralph and his assistants, they got me to my feet. Each grabbed me by an arm and helped me wobble off the field to the bench where I sat, completely disoriented and with a major headache, for the rest of the game. Later, I couldn't remember anything that had happened from the time of the collapse to the end of the game. I couldn't remember much of the bus ride back to Greencastle, either, except that I knew the trainer had been sitting next to me and from time to time had tried to make sure I wasn't asleep.

The team stopped for dinner about two hours south of Rensselaer at a family restaurant with a seating capacity of above sixty, nestled on Highway 231. The proprietor had been contacted in advance about the stop and was ready for the team. A group of fifty who would order, eat, and leave in a short time was a big deal for what was, in effect, a mom-and-pop restaurant; but at the same time, it put a lot of strain on the kitchen. For this reason, and to keep costs under control, the players could choose either fried chicken or Salisbury steak. The salad, potatoes, and vegetables were part of the meal, as was the apple pie. No special orders. I sat at a table of four with Fox, Barr, and big Ed Gardner. Everyone was happy the Tigers had won and were in good spirits, as I was, but my head really ached, and I could only pick at my food. Fox was a little sheepish at first because the St. Joseph's linebacker had delivered the hit to me and blown right by me. But it wasn't really his fault because Fox's assignment had been to seal off the inside, and because the linebacker had stayed home and came in from the outside, if anyone had blown his assignment, it had been Todd Eberle, the tight end, who was seated four tables over, stuffing his face with chicken and not giving much thought to my plight.

The team took about forty-five minutes to get through its dinner and headed back to the bus, then it was back to Greencastle. The bus stopped at the stadium and the players put their gear back into their lockers and put their washables in the laundry baskets. The uniforms went in one basket to be washed, pressed, and sown (where required) for the next away game. The jockstraps, T-shirts, and socks went in another basket and would be washed and dried for practice on Monday. The jocks, T-shirts, and socks were all the same size and were just handed out each day when a player showed up for practice. One size fit all, and usually did so quite well, except that once in a while, I knew by the fit when someone larger than me had worn something the practice before.

It was dark out when the players walked home. I walked back to the fraternity house and went directly to my room, feeling dog-tired and with a massive headache. My roommate, Morgan Everson, was back home in Indianapolis that weekend, where his girlfriend lived. It was a common occurrence for Morgan, who was very much in love, so I had the room to myself, and I fell asleep immediately.

The next day, my head still ached, although not quite as much, but I decided to have it checked out at the infirmary.

The DePauw student infirmary was run by a couple of doctors, both retired from their regular practices but hanging on to supplement their pensions and to buttress their savings. It was clear upon meeting them that their best years of practice were far behind them, but the students got used to them and trusted them with their medical needs, hoping that nothing serious requiring more than superficial medical attention would ever happen to them.

Doctor Joda, who was in his midseventies, was on duty when I walked in. On Sunday mornings, the large percentage of student noise was due to overconsumption of alcohol the night before, so the doctor was pretty surprised when I explained that my headache was related to football and not to drinking. He listened to my story and correctly concluded that I had probably experienced a concussion. He told me what a concussion really entailed and how it was to be treated, and he gave me a bottle of aspirin, telling me to use it—but not too much—if the headache persisted, and not to go back to practice until the headache stopped.

The headache would subside and then disappear over the next week, but I didn't miss any practices. I was first-string now and would not let anything, particularly just a headache, put my status in peril. I started and played the entire game against Indiana State the following Saturday without missing a beat.

Probably the only tense moment that came out of the whole experience regarding the concussion came on the Tuesday night after it had happened. I was shocked to hear on the public address in the fraternity house that there was a call from home for me. A surprise call from home often does not contain good news, so I nervously hurried to the phone room to take the call. It was my mother, and I assured her that I was one of the faster players, and even though I was smaller than most of the players on the field, they couldn't catch me in order to hurt me. For the most part, she accepted this because she went to very few games and didn't really see things for herself, relying on my accounts of the football experience.

For this call, at least, the next question was different. "Betty Hunt has a son at St. Joseph's, and she went to visit last weekend."

"Oh, yeah?" I responded. "Not much to do there. I hope she had fun."

"She went to the football game, since there was nothing else to do."

Uh-oh, I thought to myself, *I think I know where this conversation is going and I can't say I like it too much.* I remained silent.

"She said one of the DePauw players, one of the smaller ones, and I was relieved when she told me everything was OK."

Then she asked how things were and proceeded with some small talk about whether I was eating well and how my studies were going, things that are always talked about between a student and his parents when a call is made from home on a normal basis. After she reported how my brothers and sisters were doing, she asked if I had played in the game at St. Joseph's over the past weekend. This was a surprise.

My mom hated football. She described it as a bunch of boys running around a field and then falling on top of each other all afternoon, which was probably true, but she also described it as the kind of sport where someone always got hurt. That part, she really didn't like.

"Charlie, why don't you just play baseball like you did when you were younger? It was fun to watch, and you liked it. Nobody even got hurt." She had asked this question dozens of times.

I always ran with the ball, and I had gotten knocked out.

"Betty hadn't seen get the number and didn't have a program, but she'd said the player had been one of the smaller ones. Do you know who it was?"

I had long since learned that you don't lie to your mom, even when it may be better off for everyone to do so. The costs of lying to your mom, the consequences if you are caught, and the loss of trust would far exceed whatever benefit there would be in lying. You just don't do it.

"Yeah, mom. I guess it was me, but it was only for a few seconds, and I didn't get hurt. I feel great now." That last part was a lie, but not a bad one. My head still ached.

"Weren't you going to tell me?" she responded.

"I really didn't think it was worth mentioning. Guys get banged up all the time, but they bounce back and get through it. It's just football," I said.

"Just football. Just football, you say. I hate football. Nothing good happens in football; lots of bad things do, and you can't protect yourself, particularly when you are smaller than most of the players."

I had said the wrong thing. I wished I could have taken it back.

Mom continued, "Plus, it's a crummy team you played. They hardly win any games, and nobody comes to see you play. You had bigger crowds in high school." She had known at least this much about the situation.

"You are at college to study, to prepare for life and your life's work, and what are you doing while you are there? Practicing every day for games that have no meaning when you could be at the library or studying for tests, that's what. Then, to top it off, you go and get knocked unconscious to boot. Who knows what kind of damage you did to yourself that you don't know about? Why do you keep doing this? It's crazy." She really unloaded on me.

The conversation had taken place many times since I'd started playing for real in high school. I had always been careful explaining my position, and it usually worked to calm her down.

"Mom, I love the game, and it would be awful if I had to give it up when I don't want to. Everyone has some free time, and if they find a way that they think is meaningful, fun, and rewarding in which to spend it, it's good for them and for those around them. Football provides me with discipline, self-control, loyalty, and working for group goals all at the same time. It gives me a purpose and something to strive for, and these are things that few people have. Whatever I am accomplishing on the school's football team is a part of it, a big part."

I went on, "The two bad things that people hear about football are that it is an unproductive time consumption, and that a lot of people get hurt, and I don't subscribe to either one.

"I spend about three hours per day, every day of the season, and most of the day on Saturdays, which includes traveling. And that doesn't count, because people just waste time on things they like on Saturdays, and they don't do anything productive, anyhow. Sundays are off. If people were really efficient and carefully managed their time, starting and stopping an activity promptly, then moving on to the next one, they would save one or two hours a day. During the season, I don't waste time. Does playing football affect how much time I have to study? Probably some, but when I do study, I know I better do it right. No distractions, no chatting, no phone calls, so I do it better. My grades have never suffered during the football season in high school or in college, so I think that is pretty much the proof needed, at least for me.

"As for injuries, football players are well-conditioned and are taught to take care of themselves, which includes not doing anything stupid. When I block or tackle or get tackled, I usually see it coming, and I brook for it. I am prepared for the incident and can react the right way for what is coming. Sure, these is a greater chance for injury to a football player than to a chess player, but I don't like chess, and I love football, and I feel better about myself because I play it. Plus, I really like the guys on my team.

They are my friends. I would run through a brick wall for them, and they would do the same for me. We are a community that is looking out for and protecting each other.

"You and Dad have been great and have supported me all the way through school, and it has meant everything to me. You have wanted other things that you thought would be better for me, but you have let me do this, and I love you for it."

I had poured it on a little bit with my last statement. Dad liked it that I played football, and he enjoyed the opportunities to see me play, but it would not have been smart to raise this in the particular conversation that was going on.

Mom's response was surprisingly cheerful. "OK, Charlie. If it still means so much to you, keep doing it, but be careful. I don't want to get any more calls like the one from Betty Hunt. Are you absolutely sure you are OK?"

"I'm OK. I love you, and give my love to Dad."

We hung up. I figured my mother had acquiesced so quickly because she was tired of arguing with me about the subject, and because I would be involved in this foolishness for only one and a half more years before I had to tackle life's problem rather than players with numbers.

CHAPTER 40

MONON BELL
GAME, 1964

ALL HEMMED IN—Chuck (Bronco) Byrum is all hemmed in by the Wabash defense but the DePauw halfback still managed to slice through for a 3-yard gain in yesterday's Monon Bell football game at Crawfordsville. Byrum picked up 59 yards in 14 carries as Wabash won a 22-21 squeaker.

As I woke up on Saturday morning, I rubbed my eyes and looked around my room. It was the same room I had slept in for the last eight weeks since the new semester had started, but something was different. I knew it, even in my grogginess. As my faculties came back to me, I remembered the last thing I had been thinking about when I had fallen asleep the night before. This was the second Saturday in November, which was usually the date of the Monon Bell game between DePauw and Wabash, with the first big played Wabash and the string of continuous games being played since 1890. What a thrill, what an honor to play in that game. What was more, I was starting for DePauw as left halfback. I thought to myself that even if a different player started as left halfback for DePauw in the game since its inaugural in 1890, here I was, starting in 1964, one of the handful of players to do so. Maybe I was thinking too much about all that had been written about the game, and all the publicity it received, even for a small college rivalry. It was a huge event in my life. From the time I was a 140-pound halfback as a freshman, I had thought about this, never imagining it to be true that I would be starting a college game, one of the nation's oldest rivalries.

The Wabash College campus was on the outskirts of Crawfordsville, just off of Highway 231. It was a beautiful, sprawling arrangement of Georgian brick buildings, nicely spaced and planned. The campus was blessed with a number of mature oak trees with branches that were leafless in November but presented a stark contrast with a high blue sky on a cold, clear day. As the bus pulled into the football complex, a good number of Wabash students could be seen shuttling between the dorms and the academic campus, probably to go to the library for research or just for a quiet place to study. A greater number of students could be observed on the front porches and decks of the dorms and fraternity houses that circled the campus, with banners (some tasteful and some not) and kegs of beer in plain sight. Even though Wabash was an all-male school, there were plenty of women present. The campus was close to a number of coed schools, and a number of women students spent a good part of the weekends at Wabash. I thought I saw several underclass women from DePauw on the first step of one of the fraternity houses, and I was probably right.

There was a buzz in the air, the kind of tension and excitement that existed in college games, but particularly in games between old rivals. The feeling in the air was accented by the crisp temperature in the midforties and by the smell of burning leaves.

As the bus made its way through the campus toward the stadium, the revelers on the front porches shouted at the occupants in raised voices. The shouting, of course, included some vulgarities, but surprisingly enough, not that much. The verbal expressions from the front porches were more like hoots, hollers, and whistles than words. It was intense, even this early in the day, but it was doubtlessly aided by the fuel provided by the beer that had been purchased by the Wabash students.

This would be a big game, it always was, but Wabash was hungry. They had a good team this year, with a five-and-two record, and were looking to top it off with a win against DePauw. To make things more interesting, DePauw had won eight consecutive games against Wabash, which was hard for the Little Giants to accept, but the one-and-seven record of the Tigers was a big sign that the losing streak for the Little Giants could be stopped if they played a good game. The bus turned onto the driveway that led to the stadium. After a short distance, it reached the brick wall that surrounded the stadium and pulled up in front of the gate that led on the visitors' dressing room.

Just as the bus came to a stop, Coach Mont stood up from his seat in the front. There had not been much chatter among the players ever since they'd reached the campus and started taking in the sights around them, but what conversations had continued were promptly stopped.

"Men, here we are. This is the last game in what has been a long season for us. A tough season. But we have the honor of playing this game, which is one of the longest football rivalries in the United States, against a very worthy opponent. They don't care what your record is, they just want to beat you. If they win, as they expect to, it will cap off a very good season for them. If they don't, it will be a ruined season. But enough about them. What about you? What does this game mean to you? I'll tell you what it means to me. It's a new season right now. DePauw and Wabash have finished the old season with whatever records they had. We are both zero and zero right now, getting ready for the game."

Reverend Carreker, from the Methodist church at DePauw, stood up to continue speaking for Coach Mont, starting by giving the normal prayers before games. He asked for courage and heart and asked for protection from injury. Finally, he got around to asking for victory, but did so in a gentle manner, so as not to be too adamant on the subject. The Tigers were one and seven going into this year's Monon Bell game, while Wabash was five and three, so if the reverend emphasized victory too much and his prayers were not realized, it could affect his future employment. Besides, Coach Mont always had a realistic perspective on the game by reminding the team that while it was good to play for anybody, even victory, God usually listened to the prayers of the teams with the biggest tackles and fastest halfbacks.

I always liked the team breakfasts before games because steak was served, a rarity for any meal when I was growing up, but particularly for breakfast.

By 10:30 a.m., everyone had finished eating and got dressed in their uniforms, with pads and helmets stowed underneath the bus, before boarding in their seats. The thirty-mile trip usually took forty-five minutes or so, and the players were mostly silent as they sped along Highway 231 in Putnam County toward Crawfordsville. It was a rural area in Central Indiana, and there were quite a few farms along the way. The people who lived there were not urban types but were up and about their business. On Saturdays, this included a lot of burning of filler leaves, to the pungent smell of smoke-filled air, contributing to the feeling that a big game was about to be played.

I looked around the bus at the players, most of whom had fallen into their own private thoughts about the game and maybe some other things, but likely just about the game. Later in life, these players would learn to multitask and think of several subjects in one sitting, but not now. They were football players getting ready to play what was likely the biggest game of their lives, many for the last time, and their thoughts were only on the game, to the exclusion of everything else.

It was a good team, with good players and character. Like any team, it had experienced its share of injuries and had lost some players it had counted on. Of the seven games it had lost, at least half of the opposing teams had been invincible, but this hadn't had an effect on the players. They had been ready mentally, emotionally, and physically for every game, but they were more so for this one. Maybe it was because their archrival had experienced a good season, and they had not, and this was their last chance to do something about it.

Many had played before me, and many would play after me, but this was the here and now for me and all the others who would play in the game. I had put on my clothes quietly so as not to disturb my roommate, Morgan Everson, the starting forward for the DePauw basketball team, and walked into the kitchen before I got on the bus. It was 8:00 a.m., and I had surprisingly slept soundly for nine hours. I would have time for some coffee before heading over to the student union building at DePauw for the team breakfast, which was common for home games. What was not common was that this would be an away game, and after breakfast, the players would get in their game pants and game shirts and drive the thirty miles from Greencastle to Crawfordsville on the team bus with their pads and helmets stored in the equipment area of the bus, to get ready for the game. All the other away games were preceded by a bus trip on a Friday and an overnight stay in a hotel before the game, but not the Wabash game. It was different. The players slept in their own beds the night before the game, even if it as an away game.

Breakfast started at 9:00 a.m. after an invocation by Reverend Carreker, who was a little bit odd, but a nice guy. Like most clergymen who preside our team as he had done in every annual contest between two esteemed institutions that has been played many times before this.

The coach continued. "The men who played on those teams before you cared about the records of both teams, for sure, but they care most of all about what you do today. The men who played before you, for both schools, want nothing more than for their school to win today with hard play, good execution, and honor. What happens is up to you. It's in your hands. Now go get taped and dressed. We will take the field for our pregame routine in half an hour."

I sat there quietly while the coach spoke, and I experienced a surge of emotion that came from within as I heard the coach's words. They had cleared my head and focused my mind on what would happen over the next three hours. I was ready. The words had brought the effect that I was sure the coach had intended. The team quietly got out of their seats, left the bus, and entered the building containing the visitors' dressing room.

The visitors' dressing room at Wabash was old and soon to be demolished, along with the stadium, for replacement with a new, state-of-the-art facility. But for today, it was cramped and dark and smelled like hundreds of teams had used it before for taping and dressing for games, going over their strategies and adjustments before and at halftime, undressing, showering, and dressing after games. They had also used it to give speeches and pep talks in advance of games, to take injured players for treatment and attention between games, and to go through the emotional experiences relating to the outcome of the game that had just been played. Jubilation, relief, sorrow, anger, and all of the human feelings in between—not to mention apprehension, fear, and sympathy for teammates and opponents who had been injured during the game, some seriously. *These locker rooms had seen a lot*, I thought, after I had returned from getting my ankles taped in the training room and started putting on my pads.

As soon as everyone was dressed, the team took to the field for the pregame ritual. This took place starting about forty-five minutes before kickoff. The stadium was just starting to fill, and the fever pitch of the teams running out of the locker rooms to the sounds of the band and the throaty cheers for the fans would not take place until just before game time. It was a chance to get the kinks out of their systems and the butterflies out of their stomachs before game time.

The captains—Bill Alcott, Stu Young, and Ole Thomas—led the team in some calisthenics exercises for a few minutes. Then the linemen went to the far north end of the field where they squared off against each other in one-on-one blocking drills while a couple of centers who could snap the ball and the team's two punters went to the other end of the field with the backs. The centers would take turns snapping the ball to a punter who would kick the ball downfield to the backs, who were waiting in pairs. One would call for the ball, and the other would let him know where the downfield tacklers were coming from.

Finally, the coach blew the whistle, and the team broke up into three sets of eleven players. The first set was the first team offense; the second was the second team offense, including a couple of defensive players; and the third was a group comprised of defensive players. They took turns running offensive plays as a group. The reason for the mix and match made up of the units after the first team offense was that under NCAA rules in 1964, only thirty-three players could make the traveling team, so it was not possible to run a true second team offense, much less a third team or a referee, even when any other mortal would have given in to the temptation to do so. He was a true professional, and he had earned the respect of his players and his peers. When he spoke to his players, they stopped and listened. Even if they didn't always believe what he said, they believed he had earned his right to say it and to be respected for it.

"Men," (he stated all of his talks by referring to his players as men), "for a lot of you, this will be your last football game for DePauw or any other team. For the rest of you, it will be the last time you will play with some men who have been teammates and friends over the years; the Bill Alcotts, the Stu Youngs, the Ole Thomases," he said while pointing to his three senior captains.

"You will each go on from here when it is time to do so, and you will make your mark along the way. I know it because I know you, and who you are, and what got you here."

Coach is just getting warmed up, I thought.

"You are here because you love football. You love and respect the game, and those who play it, and what it means to you. There are other schools in the state of Indiana; the Notre Dames, the Purdues, where they play in front of crowds of fifty or sixty thousand in beautiful stadiums, and they have their educations fully paid for. You do not have that. There are any number of reasons why you did not play for those schools. You may be a step too slow, a couple of inches too short, or a few pounds too light. You might not be able to throw a ball or catch a ball as well as the players at these schools. This doesn't mean you shouldn't play. All it means is that you shouldn't play for them. When you block a man so he can't tackle your teammate, or when you tackle a runner when he is about to break free. When you kick the ball downfield or block the other team's kick, you are playing football—college football—and it doesn't matter to you whether you are playing in front of five thousand people or fifty thousand people. Plus, you are students. You have come to this school, one of the nation's finest, to further your education and to compete with the best. Even if you never played a down in college, you would take this with you."

He continued, "Today, you are playing the team from Wabash College. Players a lot like you. From good families, from good high schools, all paying the price to be here. They, too, will leave their school having made their marks while they were there, in the classroom and on the playing field. They, too, will be playing for the alumni of their school, pulling desperately as we stopped on the field. Wabash Nation was unleashed before me."

I, like the other members of the Tiger team, showed nothing but a look of disdain on my face. *Hooligans and lowbrows, and loud and obnoxious as this*, I muttered to myself, but inside, I was impressed with what he'd said.

The Wabash team was a good one, and their consistent success over the years on the football field was partially attributed to the fact that they ran their plays for the single-wing formation. I was familiar with it because that's the formation that my high school had ran, also with a lot of success. The single wing had an unbalanced line with the two tackles on the same side of the center and a direct snap from the center, one to me and two backs who was deep in the backfield. These two were also the main runners, and one of them—the tailback—was the main passer. The quarterback, who also called the plays and shouted out the signals, almost never touched the ball, but instead, was a blocker leaving the blocking and running capacity of the strong side loaded. Since teams rarely saw the single wing except when they played Wabash, it was tough for them to proceed for it. It was a tricky formation to run and to execute against the scout team, on the third-string, which ran the offense of the upcoming opponent in practice, just as anticipated.

After the three teams ran plays for about five to seven minutes, Coach Mont blew his whistle, and the whole team ran to the sideline then walked to the dressing room where each player sat on the stool or the bench, waiting for the coach to speak his words of inspiration.

Tommy Mont was not a polished speaker by any means. He was a football coach, and he talked like one. He was simple in his delivery, direct and straightforward. While he made it a point to keep his distance from the players, as any coach wanting to maintain the respect and control of a team will do, he was human and was not afraid to let his players know that side of him. He had paid his dues and earned his pedigree. A major college start at Maryland; an NFL quarterback, backing up Sammy Baugh with the Redskins; a college coach for many years, waiting for his opportunity; and finally, a head coach for Maryland, taking them to the Orange Bowl one year. When his time had come and gone at Maryland, which eventually happens to all coaches, he wound up at DePauw, far from the headlines and the TV appearances, but a credit to his school and a credit to the coaching fraternity. For the three years that I played for him, I never saw Coach Mont belittle a player on either team, the coach of the other team sideline, I saw a sea of red.

The school colors for Wabash were red and white, but pure red with white lettering was the blend of choice for the Wabash supporters with the white part usually relegated to a *W* on a red cap or a red sweatshirt. The visiting school usually got a modest ticket allotment in college football games, but at Wabash, playing DePauw for the Monon Bell, DePauw's ticket allotment, which was pretty puny, and the DePauw ticket holders were in the seats on the DePauw side of the field, between the two twenty-five-yard lines. The DePauw colors of black and gold could only be seen in these areas, and of the DePauw tickets, about half were sold to parents or relatives of the players, or to members of the faculty or the administration. There was a good showing by the DePauw students, but it was tame compared to those from Wabash. Their side of the field, both end zones, the standing-room area, and a fair part of the seats reserved for DePauw were occupied by students for Wabash, their girlfriends, friends, and relatives, and boy, were they loaded. *It really is pretty impressive*, I thought. *Lots of spirit, lots of enthusiasm.* It was probably fueled by a lot of hard drinks before the game and the night before, but that stuff is a part of college football. While I appreciated the spectacle of the Wabash Band playing the national anthem for a win, I remembered the now-frail old man and the student who played in the past. They, like you, are honor-bound to represent their school in the contest that will start in twenty minutes, and you must respect them for it."

"Why should you win? Why will you win, and for them? It's one word: character. They may have it, they may not. It's been a pretty easy season for them. An easy schedule. They didn't plan it that way, it just turned out that way. And no significant injuries. You, on the other hand, have played a number of tough schools, and big schools, to boot. Schools like Indiana State and Ball State, and you had played them, at last count, without six players who had been counted on to be starters this year for us. And with all of them, with your one-and-seven record, no team blew us out or ran over us. Why? Because of the character on the team."

My heart was pumping right out of my chest. I was afraid someone else would hear it.

"You can beat anyone, and you know it. You can beat Wabash, and you know it. Now, just get out there and do it. Do it for your injured teammates. Do it for those who have played before you, but mostly, just play for yourselves. You will not be able to do this forever, and you may never have an opportunity like this again. This is the last game of the season for all of you and the last game of your careers for many of you. Don't look back in ten years or fifty years with regret that you didn't give this game your all. Now, let's get out there and win this game."

The team rose to its feet in unison and let out a cheer in unison, then stampeded out of the locker room, following the three senior captains who had led them all year. The two bands, one for each school, were playing at full throttle and the crowd, about six thousand strong in total, were screaming at the tops of their lungs while the Tigers and the Little Giants charged over the field.

The football stadium at Wabash had a normal capacity of five thousand, but when the situation called for it, temporary bleachers could be set up in the two end zones and in the area on the sideline up to about the ten-yard line where the permanent seating began, bringing the total capacity to about six thousand. That's what the crowd was today, plus a few hundred more who had purchased standing-room tickets. The place was packed.

The Tigers ran across the field to the visitors' sideline to make the kickoff. Wabash lined up received the opening ball and proceeded to run it out to their twenty-five-yard line. They then got two first downs and had the ball at their own forty-five when the DePauw defense stiffened, and Wabash could only move the ball two yards in three plays. On the fourth down, Wabash punted for their forty-seven, intending to pin DePauw deep in their territory where they might make a turnover to give Wabash a good field position if they had to punt. This was a pretty good strategy.

DePauw was playing very conservatively. Bruce Mackey, DePauw's senior quarterback, had not been a starter until his senior year, but he had started all of the games in this, his senior season, and had played well. While he was a fair passer and had delivered a number of big pass plays this season, he had also thrown some interceptions at crucial times, so Coach Mont was justifiably cautious about sending in past plays with DePauw pinned so deep in its end of the field. So the Tigers ran the ball on every down. Mike Burns, the right halfback and both around 170 pound, were both fast and elusive and were good downfield blockers, but they were not of a size or a weight that would make them effective at running off-tackle plays straight into the line. Bill Alcott, our fullback, who was six feet tall, took out a couple of Wabash rushers to clear a push for me on my pass route. These were reasonable risks, and the play had at least a 50 percent chance of success if executed properly.

Mackey showed some real excitement as he called this play in the huddle. It was close to the end of the first quarter, and he had not thrown a pass yet. This would be the first one of the game. Mackey was a decent passer. He was accurate on the short ones, but his arm was average, and he couldn't throw the long ones. When he tried, he either was off the mark or he floated the ball, which made it more likely it would be intercepted. His strong suit was that he was tough and was an excellent runner for a quarterback. He wasn't particularly fast but was very shifty. He sort of jitterbugged when he ran, and with all of his feinting and cutting as he ran, it seemed that no tackler ever had a clear shot on him. That was a good thing because he was about five feet ten inches tall and weighed 170 pounds and was not built to absorb a lot of head-on pounding when tackled. He was well-suited for the Tigers, who relied on running the ball much more than the pass, and he could take advantage of the linebackers on the right side, and quite possibly, the safety with him. Mike Burns, the right halfback, was lined up in the slot, one yard off the line, between Earl and Mark Moore, the right tackle. His job was to break to the right flat, right after Earl made his own break toward the goalpost, hopefully taking the right side linebacker with him. My job from the left halfback position was to stop in place as I was going to pass block to protect Mackey from the onrushing Wabash linemen. I would hold the pass block position for the count of three, then look for a seam in the line on the left side, and once I broke through, he would cut on a forty-five-degree angle to the right and go through the spot by the right side hole vacated by the defensive back who would be chasing Liebach. There were two potential impediments to success for this play. First, the right-side defensive back might not bite on Liebach's goal pass route and might stay at home. Second, the middle linebacker might see me coming across the middle on my route and either hit me to knock me off my stride or cover large at me as I ran by. I saw the player's outstretched hand and pulled my leg back to avoid his grip. It worked. The back had grabbed only a handful of air as I ran by. With the defensive back out of the way, I scanned the field and saw it was clear. The only Wabash players in sight were those on the other side of the field who had already taken off on an angle to catch me before I got to the goal line.

I could see Coach Mont jumping up and down as I finally cut down the field and ran toward the Wabash goal line. I ran with everything I had to get as much ground as I could while the Wabash players ran across the field to cut me off. My heart pounded in my chest as I raced down the field. When I saw the Wabash backs closing in, I prepared for the blow as they knocked me out of bounds on the sideline. I was defenseless as I was hit from the side by the first Wabash player who hit me, and I cartwheeled out of bounds. I regained my feet and surveyed what was before me. The referee was already running out to the middle of the field to place the ball down on the Wabash thirty-yard line for DePauw to put it in play. The last play had covered sixty yards and had changed everything. After several possessions with no gains and punting from deep in their own territory, the Tigers were suddenly knocking on the door of opportunity at the Wabash end of the field. The crowd in the DePauw stands were delirious and screaming at the tops of their lungs. The crowd on the Wabash side sat in stunned silence.

On the very next play, Mackey, who had experienced a huge surge in confidence with his first completed pass on his first attempt, suddenly rediscovered nimbleness. He called his own number on a quarterback option play and shimmied and danced his way into the Wabash end zone. The extra point was good. Seven to nothing.

As in most rivalry games, things started to happen after the DePauw touchdown. The Wabash running game, spearheaded by Anderson, their big fullback, started to move the ball. But before they could get into the side, the right end on the wingback double-teamed the DePauw defense tackle, just like I remembered from my high school days as a wingback. This left the tailback, May, to block on the defense end, Todd Eberle. Anderson would react to May's block, going inside or outside, depending on which way May blocked Eberle. Even if May couldn't take Eberle one way or the other, Anderson could still cut off May's block, as long as May could stand Eberle up.

The signal was called, and the snap went back to Anderson. The double-team by the Wabash end and the wingback worked flawlessly to the point of the DePauw defensive tackle being knocked to a sitting position on the ground. It was up to May and Eberle and Anderson's cut. May moved to Eberle and lowered his shoulder, making contact, but Eberle got his hands up and was able to push May off-balance, driving him into the ground with his own momentum. Eberle then stepped over May's prone body and drove his shoulder into Anderson's, wrapping his arms around him.

Not much was said in the locker room at halftime. The Tigers were ahead and had exceeded everyone's expectations in doing this. They had to suffer and stop the run in the second half if they were going to win this game, and that was exactly what Coach Mont and his staff talked about during the halftime respite.

DePauw would receive the kickoff in the second half. It was extremely important to move the ball with this possession in order to take the momentum from Wabash. As the DePauw players lined up for the kickoff, expressions of resolve showed on their faces. The coach had called a return left where every player would take the man he blocked toward the middle of the field with the objective of creating a push along the left side for one of the deep return men, me and Mile Burns. No offside, no clipping, no holding. Any of these would be extremely hurtful to anything good that happened on the return. As luck would have it, two of them did. Steve Barr, a sophomore guard who started on offense and also played on the special teams, was whistled for a clip, a questionable call since a Wabash tackler pivoted and turned his back to Barr just before he was blocked, but the block clearly hit him in the back. In addition, Mike Burns, the other return man, held another Wabash player and impeded his body to tackle Mack, who had made it out to the twenty-yard line with the kick. The clipping call moved the ball back to the ten-yard line. A bad way to start the second half. Very bad. From there, DePauw started its first possession of the second half consecutively. The Tigers had worked hard to build up a lead in the first half, a lead which very few people in the stadium (and perhaps even a few on the DePauw team) did not think was possible. And they didn't want a bungled play or a turnover to give Wabash the break they so desperately needed to get back in the game, so they stuck to running plays with quick handoffs and straight-ahead blocking so as to avoid something disastrous happening. Wabash sensed this and concentrated on playing the run.

??? around Anderson legs and driving him down three yards short of the goal line.

Game over. Final score: DePauw twenty-two to Wabash twenty-one. Every player on the field would remember the game for as long as they had memories. I certainly did. I never forgot a minute of it, and would not do so for the rest of my life. I realized then, and I realize more so now, that being at the Monon Bell Game was a once-in-a-lifetime experience for any participant who had been steeped in the experience; and it always would be, for once and always, and would never be forgotten by anyone who went through it.

The Tiger lineman and Alcott, who had stayed in to block, were doing everything they could to stave off the onrushing lineman and to protect Mackey so he could make the throw. The linemen from both sides were all at least six feet two inches tall and were able to block me, at five feet eight bunches, to observe Mackey's throw.

Suddenly, over the outstretched hands of the Wabash players attempting to knock down the pass, I saw the ball floating toward me, beautifully thrown by Mackey with a perfect trajectory to come down right where I was heading, and I watched in amazement as it settled into my hands.

I instinctively tucked the ball under my arm and looked at the field ahead. The immediate threat was the defensive back on my side of the field. I was caught in a shallow position because I had run up to cover Burns in the flat, but when it became clear that the ball would not be thrown to Burns, I had instinctively backed up, but not enough. I was on a forty-five-degree angle running toward the right sideline with a full head of steam. The defensive back, while backing up, still had a bad angle, and as I ran by him, he was forced to leave his feet, and 190 pounds was best suited for these kinds of plays and was called out to run two out of every three plays. No passing, no sweeps, no cross-backs. Alcott or one of the halfback straight ahead for every play.

We will just fight our way out of this, the coach must have been thinking.

The same cycle took place three times. Wabash would run Anderson into the middle three straight plays but would not make a first down and pin back DePauw with a well-placed punt, usually inside the twenty-yard line. DePauw would return the favor and punt the ball out to midfield. Something had to give, and it did.

Wabash had been stopped again around the fifty-yard line, so they punted. This time, however, the ball could not be downed by the Wabash punt coverers, and it rolled into the end zone for a touchback. DePauw now had first and ten on its twenty-yard line, not on the ten- or fifteen-yard line that it was used to.

The offensive team ran out and huddled up on the ten-yard line, waiting for Mackey to come in with a play. He did. This time, however, rather than calling for Alcott to ran up the middle, he called for a 238 pass. When he did, it took my breath away for a split second. Wabash scored a touchdown and decided to go for two points to win by one point. This was expected in a rivalry game. No one involved in the game on either side wanted to see a tie. It could be the last touchdown of the game, and both teams were ready to roll the dice. Wabash had one play from scrimmage to get the ball out of the goal line. If they did this, they would win, being able to tell their children and grandchildren in the future that the gutsy play of their team had won the Monon Bell game. Failure to score by Wabash would mean DePauw would win. There would be no tie, and there shouldn't be in this game.

The crowd was on its feet and was yelling itself hoarse as the Wabash huddle broke and the offensive team ran up to the three-yard line where the ball was placed. They were in their regular single-wing set with May as tailback and Anderson as fullback as the quarterback called the signals. DePauw was in its regular defensive alignment with five linemen, two linebackers, a runner back, and three defensive backs, each prepared for a pass play or a running play from Wabash.

The ball was snapped by Anderson, who ran for the right. Anderson was heading for the end zone to give Wabash the win, then his eyes got bigger as he saw Eberle come out of the scrum and come at him to make the tackle. He did just that, and he hit Anderson in the gut to bring him to the ground. Down went Anderson. Game over. The Tigers won. Of the things that can be accomplished in sports, this was the sweetest ever for me and the Tigers.

The game would be the last football game I ever played, from the sandlot games at Avoca School to the college games at DePauw. Each game will be remembered for the rest of my life.

Made in the USA
Monee, IL
30 September 2023

43739958R00111